A BRIEF HISTORY OF THE DOCTRINE OF THE TRINITY IN THE EARLY CHURCH

A BRIEF HISTORY OF THE DOCTRINE OF THE TRINITY IN THE EARLY CHURCH

FRANZ DÜNZL

Translated by John Bowden

continuum

Published by T&T Clark
A Continuum imprint
The Tower Building, 11 York Road, London SE1 7NX
80 Maiden Lane, Suite 704, New York, NY 10038

www.continuumbooks.com

Translated by John Bowden from the German *Kleine Geschichte des trinitarischen
Dogmas in der Alten Kirche*, published by Verlag Herder, Freiburg, Basle and
Vienna. © Verlag Herder, Freiburg im Breisgau 2006

Translation © John Bowden 2007

British Library Cataloguing-in-Publication Data
A catalogue record for this book is available from the British Library

Typeset by Fakenham Photosetting Limited, Fakenham, Norfolk
Printed on acid-free paper in Great Britain by MPG Books Ltd, Bodmin,
Cornwall

ISBN-10: HB: 0-567-03192-6
        PB: 0-567-03193-4

ISBN-13: HB: 978-0-567-03192-1
        PB: 978-0-567-03193-8

Contents

Foreword

For a long time, there has been a need for a clear and
concise account of the emergence of the Christian doctrine
of the Trinity. The older textbooks are, for the most part,
out-of-date, giving misleading and oversimplified accounts
both of the philosophical background and the course of
the development, while the contributions of modern scholarship are often complex and lengthy, presenting a picture
very difficult for the novice theologian to take on board.
Professor Dünzl's book fills this need with a clear and
concise account of what one might call the public history of
the doctrine of the Trinity. He traces the various tributaries
to the development of the doctrine, both biblical and philosophical, with a sure touch and with lucidity. Major figures,
such as Origen, are given the attention they deserve, and
lesser figures are not neglected. The tendency of much older
scholarship, to read back into the early figures concerns that
only became apparent later, is rigorously avoided. Dünzl's
gift for clarity and concision is especially manifest in his
treatment of the fourth century, which has been the subject
of much scholarly debate for the last few decades. Without
neglecting this scholarship, he avoids the tendency to confuse
doctrinal history with the history of scholarship, leaving the
reader's head full of the wrong names (that is, the names
of the scholars, rather than the participants in the debate),
and instead concentrates on unfolding the fourth-century
story itself. The student who has absorbed Dünzl's account
will be well prepared to embark on the elaborate discussions of the late Bishop Hanson, or Simonetti, or (more

recently) Behr or Ayres. Despite his concern not to outrun the novice, Dünzl has his own contribution to make to the scholarly discussion; in particular, the role of the West and the papacy, often neglected in this context, is given careful attention, and consequently a more balanced picture of the course of doctrinal development emerges.

The history, then, is clear, concise and accessible, but Dünzl achieves more than this, for he is not just a historian, but a theologian, too. This is particularly striking in the way he presents the doctrine of the Trinity: namely, as a version of monotheism. Far from simply accepting the doctrine of the Trinity as distinctively Christian, in his initial chapters he reminds us of the fundamental affirmations of monotheism that are found in similar terms in the three Abrahamic religions. This stress on the common ground shared by Jewish, Christian and Muslim confessions is not only of real present-day relevance, but constitutes a critique of some of the currents of theological reflection that held sway in the last third of the last century, as well as representing a return to the approach to the doctrine of the Trinity found in the Cappadocian Fathers and reprised by that great epitomizer of the Greek patristic tradition, St John Damascene. Dünzl has written one of those rare books that functions both as an elementary textbook and makes a distinctive contribution to present-day theological reflection.

Andrew Louth
University of Durham

Preface

This short introduction investigates belief in the triune God, who has revealed himself as Father, Son and Spirit. Its approach is not from the perspective of dogmatics, since it is not systematic theology, but from that of church history. Nevertheless, it is essentially concerned with God's revelation or, more precisely, with the realization of this revelation in human history.

Over the centuries Christian exegesis has learned laboriously and in the face of considerable resistance to see in the biblical writings God's word in human words – often hidden like the treasure in the field, sometimes also obscured by the time-conditioned ideas of the authors, their all-too-human intentions and the limits of their language. The tradition which communicates God's revelation to us, inseparably bound up with Holy Scripture (cf. *Dei Verbum* 9), also proves to be an event deeply shaped by human effort, which can bring before our eyes both the greatness and misery of human beings.

Likewise, the confession of the triune God which was forged in a binding form at the first ecumenical councils of Nicaea (325) and Constantinople (381), and which still unites the Christian confessions today, did not fall suddenly from heaven like a meteor. Nor was it simply the self-contained legacy of primitive Christianity, which had been entrusted to the church – like Vesta's fire – merely to be preserved and protected from attacks. Rather, this confession grew out of the *living* tradition of the church in a three-hundred-year-long history, in which generations of theologians and believers took part. Passionately, acutely and often enough disputing with one another, they sought out how they could believe in the *one* God as Father, Son and Spirit. Some of the ways they took were dead ends (which have been marked out by official doctrinal condemnations and exclusion from the church community); however, it is always only after the event that it is possible to recognize where the way really leads into the future and where it gets lost in the jungles of history. Until that way had been established, the different courses taken by theologians were legitimate attempts to put their faith into words, to reflect on it and thus bring it up to date – a task which each generation of Christians faces anew.

In this book I want to depict the human struggle for the truth of the Christian image of God and, as far as possible, to allow the early Christians to speak in their own words. Those who are familiar with the material will of course know that every testimony that I include requires more technical introduction, contextualization and critical interpretation than is possible within the framework of this book. However, here my prime concern has been to bring to life the dynamic of the controversies over the theology of the Trinity and make it possible to follow them, to point out the foundations and the decisive changes of direction which determined the course of early Christian discussion, and to indicate 'outside' influences which also found their way into the theological discussion. Much will have been gained if I succeed in arousing an understanding for the historical diversity of the theological schemes and their particular concerns, and in showing that the discussion, which sometimes was carried on quite bitterly, was not just as a barren dispute but an evolutionary process in which spiritual rivalry represents a necessary and positive factor, here as everywhere, driving on the development.

I shall have achieved even more if I awaken in those who read this book an awareness that God's will is not to communicate himself by passing over human beings and without human effort. God can use the (limited) power of our thought and feelings, our (incomplete) striving for knowledge, our creativity and even our delight in disputation to disclose himself in the garb of human thoughts and words. God's aim is served not only by those theologians who advance reflection at a decisive point; God may also be served by those who go astray and provoke contradiction or correction. We can never do more than glimpse the complexity of situations. And anyone who wants to recognize something of God's plan and purpose in history will require much patience and considerable stamina.

CHAPTER 1

Introduction to the Problem

Christianity understands itself to be a monotheistic religion. How important the confession of the one and only God was is shown in exemplary fashion by a text which around 130/140 the Roman Christian Hermas put in the mouth of a revealer figure (the 'angel of repentance') as the first commandment in his lengthy work on repentance: 'First of all believe that God is one, who made all things and perfected them, and made all things to be out of that which was not, and contains all things, and is himself alone uncontained' (Hermas, *Mandate* I 1). This statement was one of the basic principles of early Christianity and was cited time and again by Christian theologians (including Irenaeus of Lyons, Origen and Athanasius of Alexandria).

With this confession Christianity is in line with the monotheistic religions related to it: Judaism before it and Islam after it. To the present day Deuteronomy 6.4 is recited daily in Jewish morning and evening prayer as a monotheistic confession of faith: 'Hear, Israel, Yahweh our God, Yahweh is one!' (cf. the words of God in Isaiah 45.5: 'I am Yahweh and there is no other; beside me there is no God!').

The first part of the Shahada, the two-membered Islamic confession of faith ('There is no God but Allah, and Muhammad is his Messenger'), takes up verses of the Qur'an (composed in the seventh century) which emphasize the oneness of God: 'God – there is no deity save Him, the

1

Ever-Living, the Self-Subsistent Fount of All Being' (Surah
2.255); 'God is He save whom there is no deity' (Surah 59.22,
23). Precisely because of its confession of the oneness of
God the Qur'an protests energetically against the Christian
doctrine of the Trinity (which had been formulated long
beforehand): 'Indeed, the truth deny they who say, "Behold,
God is the Christ, son of Mary ... Behold, anyone who
ascribes divinity to any being beside God, unto him will
God deny paradise, and his goal shall be the fire ... Indeed,
the truth deny they who say: "Behold, God is the third of
a trinity"– seeing that there is no deity whatever save the
One God ... The Christ, son of Mary, was but a messenger'
(Surah 5.72-75). From the perspective of Islam the Christian
doctrine of the Trinity is thus a dangerous error which leads
away from monotheism, although the Qur'an itself can
make amazing statements about Jesus: 'Jesus, son of Mary,
was God's messenger, His word which he had conveyed unto
Mary – and a spirit from Him' – 'nevertheless: never did the
Christ feel too proud to be God's servant ...' (Surah 4.171f.).
Here we may recognize a distant echo of the church's
Logos theology (Greek *logos* = word) or Spirit christology
(see below), which points us back to the early Christian
effort to harmonize monotheism with the significance of
Jesus for salvation and his place in the world and history, as
reflection after Easter already attempted to describe this in
New Testament times.

CHAPTER 2

The Beginnings of Christology

The catalyst and centre of this reflection is the historical Jesus of Nazareth, who during his brief public appearance (around AD 30) caused a stir with his preaching and symbolic actions in Galilee and Judaea. A group of disciples, men and women, gathered around him, accompanying or supporting the itinerant preacher. They saw him as a man who burst open the familiar categories of religious experience (teacher, wise man, mystic, prophet, charismatic, miracle worker). There was discussion about Jesus in this group; they asked *who* he could be, ventured answers and formulated hopes – probably already during his lifetime but even more after Easter, when the Jesus community gathered again and proclaimed the crucified Jesus as the Living One. There was a dramatic change when the crucified Jesus, who had died the death of a criminal cursed by God (cf. Deut. 21.23), was experienced by the witnesses to the Easter appearances as the one who had been raised and confirmed by God: this experience became the starting-point for a deepened christological reflection which persistently also shaped the image of God among the early Christians.

Here the resurrection of Jesus took on abiding significance, since it was regarded not as the conclusion but as the centre of the story of Jesus. This can be read, for example, out of the prescript (the introduction) to Paul's letter to the Romans (around 55). Using old traditional material, Paul describes the gospel of God as the message 'of his Son, who was descended from David according to the flesh and was declared to be Son of God with power according to the spirit of holiness by resurrection from the dead' (Rom. 1.3f.). In this old formula the status of Jesus is recognized twice: he is first introduced as son of David, quoting the messianic tradition according to which the Messiah is born of the seed of David – a tradition which in the Jesus tradition has been combined with the narrative of the birth of Jesus in Bethlehem (David's birthplace). But – the formula goes on – greater things can be said of him: Jesus is appointed, declared, defined (these are the nuances of the Greek verb) 'Son of God' *on the basis of* his resurrection (we could also translate this *since* his resurrection). The resurrection of Jesus means exaltation, and here exaltation is described as divine sonship.

However, christological reflection did not stop at this statement: the resurrection confirmed not only the crucified Jesus but the activity of Jesus as a whole: his preaching, his behaviour towards sinners and outcasts, his teaching and his (implicit) claim. Therefore it is only consistent that the earliest Gospel, the so-called Gospel of Mark (shortly after 70), dates the revelation of the title 'Son of God' to the beginning of Jesus' public appearance. In the scene in which Jesus submits to John's penitential baptism in the Jordan, as he rises from the water he is granted a vision: the heaven opens, the Pneuma – i.e. the Spirit of God – descends on him like a dove, and he hears a voice from heaven: 'You are my Son, the Beloved; with you I am well pleased' (cf. Mark 1.9–11). The proclamation of Jesus' divine sonship is first made to Jesus himself, but the group of those to whom it is addressed widens as the Gospel continues: the proclamation is repeated in Mark 9.7 in the transfiguration before the disciples, and in Mark 15.39 the crucified Jesus is called 'Son of God' by the (pagan) centurion of the execution squad.

The two later Synoptic Gospels ('Matthew' and 'Luke') go one step further with their infancy narratives: in their accounts Jesus does not first become the Son of God by the gift of the Spirit at his baptism in the Jordan, but from the beginning. So they tell of the miraculous birth of the Son of God from a virgin – independently of each other and in different versions. Accordingly Jesus has his origin not among human beings, but in God's initiative. For, as the evangelist writes in Matt. 1.20 (cf. Matt. 1.18), 'what is conceived in Mary is from Holy Pneuma'. And in the Gospel of Luke the angel Gabriel promises Mary: 'Holy Pneuma (Holy Spirit) will come upon you, and the power of the Most High will overshadow you, therefore the child to be born will be holy; he will be called Son of God' (Luke 1.35).

However, not even that is the last word which first-century Christians have to say on the question of Jesus. One of the greatest theologians of the earliest church, from whom the so-called Gospel of John derives, extends the perspective even wider. Granted, the *narrative* proper of his Gospel also begins with John the Baptist (cf. John 1.19ff.), but a prologue has been placed before it which does not begin at the baptism in the Jordan or even at the birth of Christ, but at the beginning of time: 'In the beginning,' says John 1.1f., 'was the Word, and the Word was with God, and the Word was God. The same was in the beginning with God.' The human being Jesus of Nazareth is not only the son of God from his birth; he is the incarnation of the Logos, the divine Word, which created all things in the beginning (cf. John 1.3 and 1.14). The Redeemer did not come into being and originate in this world, he is divine; he comes into the world from God and returns to the Father at the hour of his exaltation.

To want to interpret the pre-existence christology sketched by the Gospel of John as the culmination and end of a straight-line chronological development would, however, be to draw the wrong conclusion. For Paul in his letter to the Philippians (around 53) hands down a hymn which he himself has not composed but taken over, as exegetical research has been able to show. This hymn praises Jesus as the one who was originally in the form of God; however, he did not cling to his equality with God but emptied himself, assumed the form of a servant and became like human beings. God responded to his self-humiliation, his obedience to death on the cross, by exalting him: for at the name of Jesus every knee shall bow, and every tongue confess that 'Jesus Christ is Kyrios (i.e. Lord), to the glory of God the Father' (cf. Phil. 2.6–11). This hymn, which is older than the letters of Paul, already knows the scheme of descent and ascent which some decades later the Gospel of John develops further.

Thus already in the New Testament, which in the first and second centuries was not of course as yet a finished book but as it developed was a collection of individual writings, traditions which give very different answers to the question of Jesus of Nazareth stand side by side. So it is not surprising that different models also appear in the further christological reflection of the early church which attempt, each in its own way, to integrate belief in Jesus as the revealer and redeemer into an overall view of reality. We can easily see how, in the long run, in the competition between schemes, models of the 'high' pre-existence christology (or 'christology from above') prevail over those of a 'simple' exaltation christology (or 'christology from below'): measured by the broad perspectives of the Philippians hymn or the prologue to John's Gospel, the archaic conception of the Gospel of Mark seems modest, almost inconspicuous – anyone who proclaimed Jesus as revealer and redeemer at the end of the first century could say more and deeper things about him than the Gospel of Mark.

Nevertheless, the traces of archaic christology have been preserved in the New Testament. This is the context in which we should assess the contribution of the church theologians of the second century who gathered together the writings about Jesus Christ and in their interpretation balanced out the different christological approaches in such a way that the (apparently) homogeneous entity came into being which is familiar to us as 'New Testament'. We know some names which stand for this process: mention should be made of the martyr Justin, who was executed in Rome around 165, and Irenaeus of Lyons, who was bishop of the Greek-speaking community in this city of Gaul between 180 and 190. In their works we find for the first time traces of all four Gospels and also the other New Testament writings. Here the harmonization of the different traditions is in full swing. A pupil of Justin by the name of Tatian even created (around 170) a harmony of the Gospels, the so-called Diatessaron; probably it was originally composed in Greek and very soon translated into Syriac, and it was in use in the Syrian church down to the middle of the fifth century.

The harmonization of the New Testament traditions is an achievement of the church of the late second century. Now, thanks to historical-critical exegesis since the Enlightenment, we can look 'behind' the superficial harmony of the New Testament and perceive the exciting diversity of christological models within it.

However, the integration and harmonization of different christological ideas did not come about even in the early church without controversies. There were groups which did not go along with the overall view that arose with the collection of canonical New Testament writings, but preferred one particular tradition and rejected others. For example, the so-called Gospel of the Ebionites, only fragments of which have come down to us, indicates one such group: it must derive from second-century Jewish Christians who settled in Transjordan and called themselves 'Ebionim', i.e. the 'poor' – a title of honour which already occurs in the Psalms. This Gospel of the Ebionites presupposes the three Synoptic Gospels, but deals with them very purposefully. The infancy narratives are omitted, since the Ebionites rejected the virgin birth; for them Jesus was the son of Joseph by Mary. Instead, they attached the utmost importance to the baptism of Jesus in the Jordan and therefore handed down all the synoptic traditions at their disposal; however, they also supplemented them in accord with their own understanding (fragment 3, contained in Epiphanius, *Medicine Chest of All Heresies* XXX 13.7f.): 'Jesus also came and was baptized by John. And as he came up from the water, the heavens were opened and he saw the Holy Spirit in the form of a dove that descended and entered into him [*sic*!]. And a voice (sounded) from heaven that said: "You are my beloved Son, in you I am well pleased" (thus the edited Markan text). And again: "I have this day begotten you" ' – this clause comes from Psalm 2.7 and clearly states that the divine sonship of Jesus begins precisely on this day.

The Gospel of the Ebionites therefore presents an interpretation of Jesus which does not fall in with the harmonization of the christological concepts of all four Gospels mentioned above; rather, it emphatically insists on the concept of the Gospel of Mark, which had begun only with the baptism in the Jordan. The Gospel of the Ebionites does not take up other traditions such as the miraculous birth of Jesus or even his pre-existence; instead, it points up the Gospel of Mark even more sharply: on the day of his baptism Jesus is 'begotten' as Son of God. And he becomes Son of God by the Spirit 'entering into' him.

Because of such emphases the mainstream church regarded the Gospel of the Ebionites as heretical (whereas the Gospel of Mark itself was never suspected of heresy). The history of doctrine classifies the christology of the Gospel of the Ebionites (and related concepts) as 'adoptionism': Jesus is thought to be a mere man, but one who has been elected by God, given grace, and in this sense adopted and exalted as 'Son'. If – as here in the Gospel of the Ebionites – special emphasis is put on the fact that a divine power (the Spirit) was at work in Jesus, the term used is 'dynamistic adoptionism' (from the Greek *dynamis* = power). The representatives of such adoptionism include the leather-worker Theodotus of Byzantium, Theodotus the Younger and a certain Artemon (end of the second century).

From the perspective of a strict monotheism, the concept of adoptionism has the advantage that the elected and exalted man Jesus does not put the oneness of God in question. However, here Jesus becomes one example among many, for following in his footsteps Christians knew that they too were called by God, endowed with the spirit and elected 'sons' and 'daughters of God'. For most second-century communities the 'model' of Jesus, which to some degree represents the prototype of the Christian calling, was no longer an appropriate category with which one could convincingly describe the significance of the revealer and redeemer. In the controversy over the early-Christian image of God, adoptionism therefore remained a peripheral phenomenon.

Here I shall also leave aside alternative christologies which are to be assigned to the religious redemption movement of late antiquity known as Gnosticism. According to their concepts (which diverge markedly in details), the saviour – or, more precisely, the pneumatic (spiritual) element in him – is completely divine: he comes (as in the Gospel of John) from the sphere of transcendence but is not to be related to the Jewish creator God, who from the perspective of Gnosticism (and also that of Marcion of Sinope) is to be classified as inferior, along with his creation. The saviour represents a far higher, superior, transcendent and hidden God who fundamentally has nothing to do with the material world. In this dualistic system the Gnostic saviour did not represent any modification of belief in Yahweh (which was rejected) but its supersession; however, the controversy with Gnostic groups in the church reinforced the tendency to emphasize the oneness and sole rule (*monarchia*) of the creator God, above whom and alongside whom there could be no other – as is asserted, e.g., by Justin Martyr or Irenaeus of Lyons in the second century.

This very persistence in the confession of the one and only God of Israel confronted the early church with the task of clarifying how to define the relationship between Jesus the Son of God, in whom Christians saw more than a mere man, and this one and only God. The traditions of earliest Christianity (including the use of the title 'son') were not clear: on the one side they stated that Jesus had been sent by God to fulfil the will of the Father, that he prayed to and pleaded with his Father, set his hope on him and was raised and exalted by him; but on the other hand they also said that the divine Logos, who had been in the beginning with God, had become incarnate in Jesus, indeed that before he emptied himself the saviour was equal with God, that he is one with the Father, and like the Father can be given the titles 'Lord and God'. Statements which insinuated that the Son was subordinate to the Father stood alongside statements which emphasized the unity of Father and Son. However, this unthought-out juxtaposition of perspectives could not be satisfactory in the long term; the dynamic of christological reflection necessarily had to lead beyond it.

CHAPTER 3

First Models for the Relationship between 'Father' and 'Son'

Attempts can still be detected in the New Testament period to give a closer definition of the relationship between 'Father' and 'Son'. Different categories are used which are meant to make this relationship plausible: in the Deutero-Pauline letter to the Colossians the Son is described in a hymn as 'image of the invisible God' (Col. 1.15a). Here is a reference not only to the Pauline statement in 2 Cor. 4.4 (Christ 'is the image of God') but also to the Jewish wisdom speculation of the Wisdom of Solomon, in which personified 'Wisdom' is called the 'image of the goodness' of God (Wisdom 7.26c LXX). The category of 'image' was supremely suitable – especially in a cultural context influenced by Platonism – to express both identity and difference at the same time, since the image is not simply the original, but has a part in its identity, represents and manifests it. The same line is followed by the statement of the letter to the Hebrews that the Son is the 'reflection of God's glory' and the 'exact imprint of God's very being' (Heb. 1.3) – the Greek nouns *apaugasma* or *charakter* denote what comes about when light is radiated or reflected, or when a seal is imprinted: here too the correspondence between Son and Father is emphasized. This does not mean identity but has the consequence that in Heb. 1.8f. the Son can even be addressed as 'God' with

11

the words of Ps. 44.7f. LXX: 'Your throne, O God, is for ever and ever ... therefore O God, your God has anointed you with the oil of gladness ...' Like Col. 1.15, Heb. 1.3 also refers back to the Wisdom of Solomon, in which it is said of Wisdom that she is the 'reflection of eternal light' (Wisdom 7.26a LXX).

In the context of the two New Testament verses there is mention of the pre-existence of the Son and his mediation at creation; the Sophia-Logos speculation of Hellenistic Judaism can be recognized as the background to this. For example, the most important Jewish Hellenistic philosopher, Philo of Alexandria, a contemporary of Jesus, referred back for the representation of his view of the world both to the Old Testament Wisdom traditions, in which personified Wisdom (Greek *sophia*) plays the role of a pre-existent creative power, though one derived from God himself (cf. esp. Prov. 8.22–31 LXX), and to the philosophical concept of the world reason, the Logos, which represented a cosmic principle in the systems of the Stoa and Middle Platonism. Since Philo attempted to reconcile the biblical view of the world with Hellenistic philosophy in order to win over pagans to Jewish monotheism, in him there are the first beginnings of an identification of Sophia and Logos of the kind that later also became largely customary in Christian theology (see below). For Philo the Logos is the creative reason (*On the Creation of the World* 17, 20, 24), the totality of the ideas and forces which are at work in the creation of the world. He is God's instrument in creation, the mediator of creation, and at the same time the primal image or model of the real world. Philo designates him 'image of God', God's 'first-begotten, oldest son', and even calls him 'God', though only in a derived, not an absolute sense (*On Dreams* I 228ff.). The Logos can be regarded as a 'second (i.e. subordinate) God'. Here in the milieu of Hellenistic Judaism we come across important preconditions and stimuli for the further development of pre-existence christology, traces of which we find in the Philippians hymn, the prologue of John, and the letters to the Colossians and the Hebrews.

However, yet other attempts can be made out to describe the relationship between 'Father' and 'Son' and to express the divinity of Jesus without making him simply identical with God (the Father). The so-called 'Spirit christology', which makes use of the category of pneuma (spirit) to describe the way in which the saviour belongs to the divine sphere, is one of these attempts; it occurs in so-called 2 Clement – an originally anonymous sermon from the period between 130 and 150. This homily begins quite abruptly in 1.1 with the following invitation: 'Brothers, we must think of Jesus Christ as of God, as of the judge of the living and the dead.' The concern to express the divinity of Jesus is obvious. But how can that be reconciled with the monotheistic image of God? Chapter 9.5 gives an indication of this: 'Christ, the Lord who saved us, though he was originally pneuma (i.e. spirit), became flesh and so called us.' The subject of the statement is Christ, the saviour, who has become flesh. If it is now asked what he was before this the text gives the answer: originally he was pneuma, i.e. he belonged to the divine sphere, he was of a divine kind, just like God (the Father). One has to acknowledge Jesus as God, because in his pre-existence he was pneuma, of the same 'substance' as God (the Father) himself. Certainly the saviour can be distinguished from the Father (thus, for example, in the doxology in 2 Clement 20.5: 'Glory be to the only invisible God, the Father of truth, who sent forth to us the saviour …'), but in being pneuma the two correspond, they are the same. Behind this lies the notion that the sphere of the divine, indeed the nature of God, *is* 'pneumatic' or 'pneuma' – John 4.24 ('God is pneuma') is also (mis)understood in this sense in the early church as a statement about the nature, the substance of God. The being pneuma which binds together God (the Father) and Jesus Christ allows the specifically Christian 'extension' of monotheism.

Another variant of this model is offered at around the same time (*c.*130/140) by the so-called *Shepherd of Hermas*, a much-noted writing on the theme of repentance, though this also reveals the author's unusual christological notions: in the fifth *Similitude* of this writing Hermas attempts to describe the incarnation: 'God made the pre-existent Holy Pneuma, which created all creation, to dwell in a flesh (Greek *sarx*), which he had chosen. And this flesh, in which the Holy Pneuma dwelled, served the Pneuma well ... and did not defile it in any way. As it worked with the Pneuma in every way, behaving with power and bravery, God chose it as companion with the Holy Pneuma; for the conduct of this flesh pleased God, because it was not defiled while it was bearing the Holy Pneuma on earth' (V 6.5f.). For Hermas, Jesus is the 'flesh', the *sarx*, chosen by God. Here the Greek noun denotes the whole human being according to its nature, human nature, which is weak, frail, transitory and endangered – for individuals can prove themselves or go wrong. Jesus proved himself. But he was not just 'flesh', i.e. a frail human being; the pre-existent Holy Pneuma dwelt in him. In contrast to 2 Clement, however, here the term pneuma does not describe the nature or the sphere of God but seems to be personified: the Holy Pneuma stands for a figure in salvation history related to God which here in Hermas as mediator at creation fills the space of christo-logical pre-existence (as in other schemes does the Logos or the Sophia). Because the Christian Hermas names the Holy Pneuma in particular as the pre-existent divine entity which dwelt in Jesus, his image of God is characterized by a 'binitarian trend'. But at the same time it is again made clear that the saviour is not simply to be identified with God.

That this is one of the many tentative attempts to express the status and significance of Christ in relation to God becomes particularly clear if we note that Hermas also uses other categories for this purpose: in his *Mandates* and *Similitudes* he repeatedly speaks of a great, glorious and exalted angel or a glorious man who is occasionally also called 'angel of the Lord' (thus in *Sim.* VII 5; VIII 1.2, 5; 2.1). In some scenes he is surrounded by a crowd of other men, including six exalted on his right and on his left (cf. *Sim.* IX 6.1–2). Finally, in *Sim.* IX 12.6, 8 the whole group is interpreted: the crowd of men 'are all glorious angels; by these the Lord has been walled round ... The glorious man [in the middle] is the Son of God, and those six are glorious angels supporting him on the right hand and on the left. None of these glorious angels can enter into God's presence without him. Whoever receives not his name shall not enter into the kingdom of God.' So the designations 'glorious man' or 'exceedingly great, glorious angel', or even 'angel of the Lord', are ciphers for the Son of God, Jesus Christ, but Hermas does not mention his name explicitly at any point in his work.

If we are to be able to put all this better in context, we must keep in mind the Jewish background to the figure of the angel. The Old Testament often speaks of the angel of Yahweh, the *mal'ak Yahweh* or *mal'ak elohim* (in Greek this becomes the *angelos kyriou*, the angel of the Lord). *mal'ak* or *angelos* originally means 'messenger', so this is a messenger of Yahweh, a messenger of God. Such messengers sometimes appear in connection with an appearance of God, a theophany, and within one and the same narrative the angel of Yahweh can be identified with God and then again distinguished from him (cf. e.g. Gen. 6.7–14; Gen. 18.1–19.1; Ex. 3.2–6; Judg. 6.11–24). For example, in the scene at the burning bush (Ex. 3.1ff.) we read: Moses 'came to Horeb, the mountain of God. There the angel of the Lord appeared to him in a flame of fire out of a bush ... the bush was blazing, yet it was not consumed ... When the Lord saw that he had turned aside to see, God called to him out of the bush, "Moses, Moses!" And he said, "Here I am".' So the angel of the Lord appears in the bush, but God the Lord himself speaks from it. The angel of Yahweh is brought on the scene as a direct representative of God, the messenger represents the one who has given him his task: the two are virtually interchangeable.

This angel of the Lord cannot therefore be regarded as some servant spirit of lesser rank, but is God's direct plenipotentiary, and precisely this function is transferred to the saviour. That of course made it easy for Christians to see in the Old Testament 'angel of the Lord' Jesus Christ, *the* plenipotentiary of God, and to refer the theophanies handed down in the Old Testament to the pre-existent Christ. According to this view God the Father himself remains

transcendent; it is his Son who shows himself to the patri-
archs and Moses.

Justin Martyr emphasizes this very point around 160,
in his *Dialogue with the Jew Trypho*, which was probably
written for 'godfearing' pagans, who were wavering between
Judaism and Christianity. In his commentary on the scene
at the burning bush in Ex. 3, Justin makes it quite clear that
no one 'who has but the smallest intelligence will venture to
assert that the Maker and Father of all things, having left all
supercelestial matters, was visible on a little portion of the
earth' (*Dialogue* 60.2). Accordingly the theophany in Ex. 3
has to be interpreted differently: for Justin, the angel who
appears to Moses and God the Lord who speaks with him
are one and the same person, namely the 'minister to God,
who is above the world, above whom there is no other [God]'
(*Dialogue* 60.5). The same is true of the other theophanies of
the Old Testament: 'Neither Abraham, nor Isaac, nor Jacob,
nor any other man, saw the Father . . . but [saw] him who was
according to the will of the Father God, his Son, and Angel
because he ministered to his will ...' (*Dialogue* 127.4).

The notion that Christ knows the will of the Father,
who remains absolutely transcendent, fulfils that will and
proclaims it to men and women, and in this way 'ministers'
to the Father, is decisive for this angel christology (which,
as is evident in Justin here, does not need to stand in the
way of the title God for Christ). The element of subordination present in this conception (and in the title 'angel')
is not at all unusual for early Christianity – it corresponds to the perspective of salvation history, the economy
(Greek *oikonomia*), which already shapes the New Testament
writings.

Oikonomia originally means the administration of a
household, and then also more generally the administration
of a city or state, or administration generally – hence the
present-day term economy. Already in Greek philosophy
– more precisely in the school of the Stoa which was founded
in 300 BC and exercised great influence in the imperial
period – the term oikonomia was extended to the divine
rule of the world. The world is interpreted as a great house

(Greek *oikos*), for which the deity provides the administration. The Christians also took over this understanding.
They use oikonomia to designate God's saving plan and
its implementation in salvation history. And in their view
Christ, the Son of God, is the most important agent in this
saving plan, the mediator of salvation. The Holy Spirit, the
Pneuma, appears alongside him. God (the Father) carries
out his saving plan through Son and Spirit – already in the
creation and in the Old Testament theophanies, but then
even more in the incarnation and the sending of the Holy
Spirit.

Around 185, Bishop Irenaeus of Lyons uses a very vivid
picture for this perspective from the economy of salvation:
for him Son and Spirit are the two 'hands of God', so to
speak the executive organs of his will, which of course both
belong to 'God himself'. The background to the anthropo-
morphic talk of the hands of God is the Old Testament; the
application to God, Father, Son and Spirit, is prepared for
by an early Christian theologian, Theophilus of Antioch,
but it is first carried through consistently in Irenaeus (cf. e.g.
Against the Heresies IV, pref. 4; 20.1; V 1.3; 5.1; 6.1; 28.4 and
Demonstration of the Apostolic Preaching 11). So there is a fixed
order in the economy of salvation: the origin and goal or
final authority of creation, redemption and consummation
is the Father, God in an absolute sense. But the real 'work' of
salvation history is done by the Son and the Spirit, who serve
the Father but at the same time are 'organically' related to
him. No decision is made about the ontological status of Son
and Spirit – this question is not raised here.

Instead, in his works Irenaeus of Lyons illustrates his view
of the oikonomia: in respect of the creation of the world he
writes in his *Demonstration of the Apostolic Preaching* 5: 'And,
since God is rational (*logikos*), therefore by the Word (the
Logos) he created the things that were made (cf. John 1.3);
and as God is spirit (*pneuma*) (cf. John 4.24), by the Spirit
(the *Pneuma*) he adorned all things; as also the prophet
says: "By the Word (the Logos) of the Lord were the heavens
established, and by his Spirit (*Pneuma*) all their power" (cf.
Ps. 32.6 LXX).' The differentiated activities of Logos and

Pneuma at creation (creating and adorning) are described in yet more detail in what follows: the Logos 'makes bodily' and 'bestows the power of existence', the Pneuma 'orders and forms the differences of forces'.

At another point (in *Heresies* IV 38.3), Irenaeus describes God's saving plan with human beings in a comparable way, when he emphasizes that the created human being in a quite definite 'order ... becomes the image and likeness (cf. Gen. 1.26) of the uncreated God, in which the Father approves and commands, the Son works and shapes, and the Spirit nourishes and makes grow'. In this triadically differentiated process God the Father appears as initiator, but he can just as well be introduced as the goal and crowning conclusion of salvation history: 'The Spirit prepares men and women for the Son of God, the Son leads them to the Father, the Father bestows incorruptibility for eternal life which each individual gains by seeing God' (*Heresies* IV 20.5).

Irenaeus is not alone in having this 'economic' perspective; it can be demonstrated that the idea of a collaboration between the triad 'Father – Son – Pneuma' in salvation history finds linguistic expression over a broad spread of early Christian literature in the later second century and the beginning of the third. The special character of this theology is to be seen in the way in which it can depict unity and distinction within the triad and the relationship of the three entities to one another in their activity which can be experienced within the world or is handed down by tradition, and in their manifestation to human beings, without reflecting on them abstractly or 'metaphysically'.

It is therefore difficult for us to commandeer Irenaeus and some other theologians of his time for a polished and clearly classifiable concept of the Christian idea of God. That would be too forced. Indeed, firm answers to the question how belief in the one and only God can conceptually be reconciled with talk of (God) Father, Son and Spirit (which increasingly played a central role in the liturgy of baptism: cf. Matt. 28.19; *Didache* 7.1, 3; Justin, *First Apology*

61.3, 10-13; Irenaeus, *Heresies* III 17.1 and *Demonstration* 3, 6-7; Tertullian, *On Baptism* 6; 13.3 etc.; *Apostolic Tradition* 12) presuppose that the problem as such had been formulated and that debate on it had opened.

However, the posing of this particular set of problems seems to have been achieved in the late second century. We find an example of this in the Apologist Athenagoras of Athens, who in his *Supplication on behalf of Christians* around 177 sought to defend Christians against the charge of atheism. To this end in chapter 12 of this apologia he points out how important knowledge of God is for Christians and illustrates this theological interest with the following questions: 'In what does the unity of the Son (Greek *pais*) with the Father consist, in what the community of the Father with the Son, what is the Pneuma and in what does the union of those mentioned and the differentiation of those thus united consist?' These questions not only raise the central problem of the doctrine of the Trinity, but Athenagoras also describes the two poles which must be taken account of in the solution of the problem (namely the unity and distinction of Father, Son and Pneuma). He also provides a specific vocabulary as a tool for theological reflection when in chapter 10 he states that Christians could both demonstrate the 'power' of God the Father, God the Son and Holy Pneuma 'which consists in the union, and also their distinction, which is grounded in the order'. Accordingly power (Greek *dynamis*) is regarded as a point of unity of the divine triad, whereas their differentiation is made plausible as (gradated) order (Greek *taxis*) in the sense of the economy of salvation.

The awareness of the problem in the theology of the Trinity which here becomes explicit with Athenagoras can be regarded as an indication that such questions were increasingly rife among Christians. There were no ready-made solutions to which reference could have been made; they first had to be achieved laboriously through discussion about one's own (biblical) traditions and the help of models of understanding for metaphysical questions available in the environment of Christianity. That here divergent schemes could compete, and time and again led to bitter theological disputes, is amazing only from the perspective of a long-established doctrine of the Trinity which is taken for granted.

CHAPTER 4

The Controversy between Logos Theologians and Monarchians

In the later second and third centuries the question how the saviour as 'Lord and God' (cf. John 20.28) can be integrated into monotheism was not only a problem within the church but also played a role in the Christian mission, as it came into open competition with (Diaspora) Judaism and was aimed at the same target group (sympathizers with a monotheistic view of God, biblical ethics and the hope of salvation). The wooing of this target group becomes evident in the fictitious *Dialogue with the Jew Trypho* which Justin Martyr wrote in Rome around 160 in order to refute objections to Christian faith and practice which could be brought from the Jewish perspective. He puts such a serious objection in the mouth of his Jewish conversation-partner in *Dialogue* 48.1: 'For your assertion that this Christ existed as God before the ages, that he then submitted to be born and become man, yet that he is not man of man, appears to me to be not merely paradoxical, but also foolish.' Justin counters this by formulating the aim of his christological argument in *Dialogue* 56.11 as follows: 'I shall endeavour to persuade you that he who is said to have appeared to Abraham and to Jacob and to Moses, is an additional God to him who made all things – [distinct] numerically, I mean, not [distinct] in will. For I affirm that he has never at any time done or said anything which he who made the world – above whom there is no other God – has not wished him both to do and to engage himself with.' Justin's fictitious conversation-partner is not the only one to be alienated by the notion that an 'additional God' should be subordinate to the 'creator God', but we already know Justin's theological motive for safeguarding the transcendence of the supreme God and attributing the Old Testament theophanies to the pre-existent Christ from the so-called 'angel christology' (see above, Chapter 3). Nevertheless the 'counting' of two Gods (who of course correspond in will) remains offensive from a strictly monotheistic perspective. In order to make this notion plausible nevertheless, Justin resorts to the Logos christology, which has its roots not only in the prologue to the Gospel of John but also in Greek philosophy.

The Greek term *logos* is derived from the verb *lego*, the basic meaning of which is usually rendered 'say, speak'. However, this does not mean just the process of speaking. The verb *lego* implies more (as in the English 'lay open'): it denotes the content, meaning and rationality of a statement. Thus *logos* denotes not merely word or speech, but also the intellectual content or the meaning of a discourse or teaching generally. The term also denotes the inner logic of a matter, its rationality and reasonableness, and therefore *logos* can also be translated as 'reason'. The spectrum of meaning of the term is thus quite broad and comprehensive.

Long before Christ the term had become important for Greek philosophy. Around 500 BC the pre-Socratic philosopher Heraclitus of Ephesus, nicknamed 'the Obscure', had discovered the ultimate principle of the world in the Logos. Heraclitus's philosophy was influenced throughout by the permanent change in the world: everything is in flux; nothing remains as it is; there is a constant conflict and war between the opposites, yet behind all change, behind all opposites and behind all dispute there is an ultimate which binds together in a harmonious unity all that is contradictory, namely the Logos. It is the law of the world, the impersonal world reason which guides and directs everything and produces the dialectical change of opposites (like coming into being and passing away). However, this Logos remains largely hidden from human beings, although their soul has a share in the Logos, in reason. They are to strive to know the universal Logos, then they will also understand the contradictory world; instead of this, most follow only their own limited views and in so doing always remain merely ignorant objects in the play of opposing forces. The pre-Socratic Heraclitus succeeded in combining the confusing diversity and contradictory nature of the world in the term Logos to form a unity which is accessible to reason, to philosophy.

That is how the term Logos was introduced into the history of philosophy. It was then disseminated very widely by the Stoa, a philosophical school which had been founded around 300 BC by Zeno of Kition. According to Stoic teaching, the world is a living whole, a mighty organism, all parts of which are permeated by the divine Pneuma (Spirit), which as the finest matter holds the universe together. When the Stoics wanted to express their intuition that the cosmos is not an irrational whole which vegetates without meaning and purpose, they too resorted to the concept of the Logos. As world reason the Logos pervades the whole cosmos; it consists of subtle material Pneuma – accordingly the Pneuma which permeates everything is the matter of the Logos, but the Logos itself is the rational principle according to which the world is built up and by which it is directed. Human beings, too, are endowed with Logos and should strive to live in accordance with the world-Logos; to do this they must above all overcome their emotions. The Stoics called that share in the material world-Logos which is part of the human constitution a person's inner Logos (Greek *logos endiathetos*); the Logos which is expressed (the *logos prophorikos*), the Logos brought forth, i.e. human linguistic expression, is to be distinguished from this. This distinction was also to become important for the Christian Logos concept.

Thus the Stoa had taken up and developed ideas of the philosopher Heraclitus. In so doing it also influenced Middle Platonism, since of course the philosophical schools did not exist in sterile isolation from one another but lived side by side in lively exchange and competition. The Platonists named the highest spiritual principle the Nous, by this denoting the absolute transcendence, the pure Intellect, which as a matter of course they thought to be purely immaterial. But the Nous first has an effect on the world through the Logos, which is its active energy. It mediates between the pure Intellect and the world and stands at the point of transition from transcendence to immanence, from absolute unity to diversity. In the predominant philosophical view of the world in late antiquity the Logos is thus given a mediating function between the pure Intellect, which rests untouched in itself, and the diverse cosmos.

This particular concept of mediation between transcendence and immanence had already fascinated the Hellenistic Jew Philo of Alexandria, who had sought to produce a balance between biblical theology and Greek philosophy; it likewise fascinated Christians interested in philosophy, such as Justin, who takes up this concept in *Dialogue* 61.1f.: 'As the beginning before all creatures God begat of himself a certain rational power (Greek *dynamis logike*)'; in scripture this rational power is among other things sometimes called 'Son, again Wisdom, again Angel, then God, and then Lord and Logos ... For he can be called by all those names, since he ministers to the Father's plan and was begotten of the Father by an act of will.' Now Justin wants to make the begetting of the Logos from the Father plausible to his readers: 'We see something similar happening among us (human beings): when we bring forth a Logos (i.e. a word or discourse) we beget a Logos without anything being separated from us by this bringing forth, so that the Logos in us (i.e. reason) is in no way diminished.' This explanation is based on the Stoic notion of the inner Logos and the expressed Logos (the *logos endiathetos* and the *logos prophorikos*). It is similar, Justin wants to say, with God: God has his Logos, his reason and wisdom, in himself, and all that does not become less when he brings forth the Logos as power. This divine Logos mediates the will of the creator of the world in salvation history without damaging the creator's transcendence – a notion which is indebted to the philosophical concept of God.

However, not all theologians of the early church shared this philosophical concept of God. Some also looked with mistrust and scepticism on the 'dogma' of the absolute transcendence of God, which required the introduction of an additional God as mediator with the world and history, and instead attached importance to remaining true to their own biblical tradition; that meant first and foremost fidelity to strict monotheism, the Jewish legacy in Christianity. The early Christians did not yet have the word monotheism, but used a different term, namely 'monarchy' (*monarchia*). They spoke emphatically of the 'sole rule of the one God', of the divine monarchy. In principle that was true of *all* Christians, but these included theologians who fought for or defended this principle with special verve.

That becomes all the more understandable when we remember that the church had first waged, and was still waging, a defensive war against Gnosticism, that redemptive movement of late antiquity which translated the Christian message into a Platonizing dualism and assigned the saviour who communicates the knowledge (*gnosis*) that brings salvation not to the creator of the material world (the God of the Jewish Bible), but to an unimaginably higher, completely transcendent, deity who through gnosis wants to liberate the innermost spiritual 'sparks' in human beings from being lost in error and ignorance and being imprisoned in matter.

Against such attempts to split reality up into an inferior material realm, which is to be attributed to the limited, ignorant God of the Old Testament, and the fullness (Greek *pleroma*) which has brought forth the saviour in order to lead back the sparks of light dispersed in the world, church theologians set the confession of the sole rule of the one God who has created the *whole* world (visible and invisible) and redeems and brings to consummation the *whole* human being, body and soul. For the anti-Gnostic theologians, the God of redemption is none other than the creator God of the Old Testament. They saw this conviction already expressed in the holy scriptures of the Jewish people (which they read in the Greek Septuagint/LXX translation) – thus e.g. in Isa. 43.11: 'I, I am the Lord, and besides me there is no saviour'; even more clearly in Isa. 63.8f.: 'And he [the Lord] became their saviour in all their distress. It was no messenger or angel but his presence that saved them; in his love and in his pity he redeemed them ...'; or Baruch 3.36–38: 'This is our God; no other can be compared to him. He found the whole way to knowledge, and gave it to his servant Jacob, and to Israel, whom he loved. Afterward he appeared on earth and lived with humankind' – this statement was recognized as a prophecy of the incarnation in the early church.

The church's opposition to the tearing apart of creation and redemption, spirit and matter, and the anti-Gnostic emphasis on the sole rule of the one God were expressed in sketches of the Christian image of God. Hippolytus of Rome hands down one such sketch in his *Refutation of all Heresies* (around 225), namely the teaching of a certain Noetus of Smyrna, who was probably bishop of that city in the second half of the second century. Hippolytus rejects this theology, but he does not seem to have given a bad description of Noetus' teaching. According to it: 'There is one Father and God of the universe, and he made all things, and was imperceptible ... as long as he might so desire, but then appeared when he wished; and he is invisible as long as he is not seen, but visible whenever he is seen. And he is unbegotten as long as he is not generated, but begotten when he is born of the virgin; so too he is not subject to suffering and immortal as long as he does not suffer and die, but when he has taken on suffering, he suffers and dies' (*Refutation* X 27.1–2). Noetus' concern emerges clearly from these lines: he is concerned about the oneness of God, about the identity of creator and saviour, and about the compatibility of transcendence and immanence in the Christian image of God. The one God is both invisible and visible, unbegotten and begotten, incapable of suffering and capable of suffering, immortal and mortal. This paradox maintains the philosophical concept of a purely spiritual, absolutely transcendent, divine being on the one hand, but on the other hand transcends it in concepts of the Bible and salvation history.

At another point (*Refutation* IX 10.11) Hippolytus describes how Noetus or his followers thought about the incarnation and thus also about God the Father and God the Son: 'As long as the Father was not begotten or born, he was rightly called the Father; but when it pleased him to submit himself to birth, through birth he became his own Son, not the son of another ... What is named Father and Son is in reality one and the same; that is not one from another, but himself from himself, by name called Father and Son, depending on the change of times. It is one who appeared there and submitted to birth from the Virgin and walked as man among men; to those who saw him he made himself known as Son because of the birth that took place; but he is the Father and has not hidden it from those who could grasp it.' According to this doctrine the terms 'Father' and 'Son' do not indicate any real difference; rather, one and the same God is characterized in different ways depending on circumstances. The term 'Son' fits the incarnate one because here God is *born* and thus is visible and capable of suffering. The name 'Father' applies to God in so far as he is *unbegotten*, invisible and incapable of suffering (and remains so despite the incarnation). The names 'Father' and 'Son' merely show so to speak different modes of being (Latin *modi*) of the one God – for this reason the term 'modalistic Monarchianism' has become established in the history of doctrine for the teachings of Noetus and his disciples.

The statement of the Monarchians around Noetus that the Son has revealed to those who could grasp it that in truth he is the Father, is worth noting. For in the Gospel of John there are passages which have been interpreted in a Monarchian sense – for example Jesus' saying in John 10.30, 'I and the Father are one'; or John 10.38, 'You will know and understand that the Father is in me and I am in the Father'; at even greater length in John 14.8–10: 'Philip said to Jesus: "Lord, show us the Father, and we will be satisfied." Jesus said to him: "Have I been with you all this time, Philip, and you still do not know me? Whoever has seen me has seen the Father. How can you say, 'Show us the Father?' Do you not believe that I am in the Father and the Father is in me?" '

Didn't such texts clearly support the theology of Noetus and his disciples?

At all events, it is clear that with such a theology the monarchy of God in the strictest sense gained currency. Here Jewish monotheism remained impressively preserved, except that the God of the Old Testament has appeared as a human being in Jesus Christ, he has suffered as a human being and has redeemed us. That is not complicated trinitarian speculation but a clear, understandable doctrine, *the* alternative to Gnostic dualism and pagan polytheism. It is quite imaginable that in the second century, at least in Asia Minor, such modalism was common church teaching.

The situation was first complicated by the export of this Monarchian doctrine also to the great cultural metropolises of the empire, so that it reached Rome, Alexandria or Carthage. For the Logos theologians with their philosophical orientation – for example Justin, who had established his school for Christian philosophy in Rome, or Hippolytus – taught there. So in the great cities the two theological tendencies met, and there was a confrontation.

First of all the names of the adversaries involved need to be given, so far as they have been preserved. His deacon Epigonus brought the teaching of Noetus to Rome; Epigonus's disciple Cleomenes then also worked there and built up a Monarchian school at the beginning of the third century; the Roman bishop Zephyrinus and his deacon and later successor Callistus are said to have supported him. A certain Sabellius also joined this group; he later attained such fame that in the mainstream church the modalistic heresy was defamed as 'Sabellianism'. We know all these names through the anti-heretical writer and Logos theologian Hippolytus of Rome, who in his *Refutation of all Heresies*, which has already been mentioned, also fought against the Monarchians. Somewhat later (around 240) the Roman presbyter Novatian also attacked this theological group in his writing *On the Trinity*.

In addition, at the beginning of the third century a certain Praxeas disseminated modalistic Monarchianism in Rome and Carthage. In Carthage, however, he came up against the most skilled opponent of this theory, the Logos theologian Tertullian, who composed a work specifically directed against him, *Against Praxeas*. There were also controversies over Monarchianism in the East. The text of a disputation has been preserved in which the famous theologian Origen, who came from Alexandria, endeavoured to deter a Bishop Heraclides from getting dangerously close to the theological position of the Monarchians. Origen himself had developed the doctrine of the divine Logos extensively.

Of course the adversaries immediately saw each other's weak points: in the great cities the Monarchians came up against Christian theologians who named another 'God' alongside God the Father of the universe, namely the Logos. And these theologians firmly distinguished the God Logos from God the Father, by number. That gave the Monarchians good ammunition. They saw the monarchy of God surrendered, and forthrightly called their opponents 'ditheists' (adherents of two gods). Conversely, the Logos theologians immediately put their fingers on a weak point of Monarchian doctrine, for the logical consequence of this radical belief in one God had to be that God the Father had himself suffered on earth – hence the Monarchian Christians were also mocked as 'Patripassians'.

Thus both sides exaggerated the teaching of their opponents polemically to an intolerable degree. For in this dispute and over wide stretches of the history of doctrine the specific issue was: what could be said with good reason about God and Christ without causing offence and what could not?

The criticism of opponents had an effect on the doctrine of both sides: the Logos theologians in no way understood themselves as ditheists and sought to defend themselves against this charge, and the Monarchian Christians equally disliked the charge of Patripassianism. Therefore the Monarchians attempted to make their doctrine more precise. They now began to distinguish the terms 'Father' and 'Son' more clearly than before: if according to the conviction of the church Jesus Christ is God and man at the same time, then concretely the term 'Son' denotes the human element in Jesus and the term 'Father' the divine element. The Monarchians could also express this with the help of the terms *pneuma* (spirit) and *sarx* (flesh): in Christ there is human and divine; the characteristic of the human is the *sarx*, the flesh, but the characteristic of the divine is the divine *pneuma*, the spirit. The flesh (in the sense of the whole human being) which is capable of suffering is the Son, but the divine *pneuma* which has dwelt in this flesh since the incarnation is the Father who is incapable of suffering. That means that the Father himself does not suffer at the crucifixion, because it is not the divine *pneuma* that suffers but the human *sarx*. However, because the Father dwells in the *sarx* as divine *pneuma*, the Father takes part in the suffering of the flesh. So here an effort is made to tone down Patripassianism, though it could not convince the Monarchians' opponents.

The reaction of the Logos theologians to Monarchian teaching can best be demonstrated through the Carthaginian Christian Tertullian, who in his treatise *Against Praxeas* (*c.*210) not only sought to refute it with exegetical perspicacity and polemical sarcasm but also presented the first sketch of a theology of the Trinity which is really worthy of the name.

Tertullian bases himself (in *Praxeas* 9f.) first on the logic of language: for him 'Father' and 'Son' are designations of a relationship for which *two different* entities are needed; I cannot be my own father or my own son. However, Tertullian knows the objection that the Monarchians will now make: 'With God, nothing is impossible. Had he so willed, he could have made himself into his own Son.' Now Tertullian does not want to put the omnipotence of God in question, but he requires proof that God *really* willed and did what the Monarchians teach. To get that, one has to resort to the Bible as the decisive point of reference by which truth or error can be measured.

In the Bible Tertullian finds instances of the distinction between Father and Son, e.g. in Ps. 2.7, a proclamation of God which the church refers to Christ: 'You are my son, today I have begotten you.' But where can one read what the Monarchians think, 'I am my son, today I have begotten myself', or 'Even before the morning star I have begotten myself' (cf. Ps. 109.3 in the LXX), or 'I have created myself as the beginning of my ways to my works ... even before the hills I have begotten myself' (cf. Prov. 8.22, 25)? With such irony Tertullian demonstrates in *Praxeas* 11 that the Monarchian theory lacks a biblical foundation, since of course there are no such scriptural passages.

Tertullian also questions the scriptural proofs which seem to support the Monarchians (in *Praxeas* 20–26). The most important are the passages from the Gospel of John which have already been quoted, in which the Johannine Christ himself speaks of his relationship to the Father, namely John 10.30, 'I and the Father are one', and John 14.9f., 'Whoever sees me, sees the Father', or 'I am in the Father and the Father is in me.' In connection with these verses Tertullian criticizes the heretics' usual practice of tearing particular biblical statements from their context and orientating everything else on them. Precisely that, he says, is also the case here: in the whole of the Gospel of John there are only three statements which can be interpreted in a Monarchian way. All the rest of the Gospel contradicts Monarchianism. In the very first two verses we read: '... and the Logos was with God ... In the beginning he was with God.' The one who was *with* God must surely be another than the God *with whom* he was. In a later chapter Jesus points out that according to the law of Moses the testimony of two witnesses is valid, and continues: 'I am the one who bears witness about myself, and the Father who sent me also bears witness to me' (John 8.17f.). But that makes sense only if Son and Father are two *different* witnesses. Tertullian works through the whole of the Gospel of John in a similar way (cf. *Praxeas* 21–25).

But there are still the 'Monarchian' verses quoted above. The trickiest problem is posed by the apparently clear statement 'I and the Father are one' (John 10.30) – but as a skilled exegete Tertullian is able to get round this (cf. *Praxeas* 22.10–13). He remarks that the plural 'we are' (Latin *sumus*) should already raise suspicions. Moreover what is written is not 'I and the Father are one person (masculine,

Latin *unus*)' but 'I and the Father are one (neuter, Latin *unum*)'! Thus the verse is quite evidently not focused on the singular (one person), but on the unity, the similarity and the bond between Father and Son, on the love of the Father for the Son and the obedience of the Son to the Father's will. The other Monarchian key passages also point to this unity in will and activity.

However, Tertullian does not limit himself to refuting his opponents; he also formulates the trinitarian counter-position. With him for the first time we find a systematic *theory* of the economy of salvation, i.e. that order or that plan according to which God the Father implements the salvation of human beings with the help of the Son and the Holy Spirit. The oikonomia, says Tertullian (in *Praxeas* 2.4), develops the divine unity into a trinity. It defines Father, Son and Spirit as three. However, they are not three in status, i.e. in the state of being, but three in their gradation. Nor are they three by substance, but three by their particular forms. Nor, again, are they three by power, but three by their specific expression. For it is from one God that these grada-tions, forms and specific expressions are derived under the name of the Father and the Son and the Holy Spirit. Thus according to Tertullian there is only one God, only one divine state of being or status, only one divine substance and one divine power. But in salvation history, in creation and redemption different gradations, forms and specific expres-sions of the deity can be distinguished, namely the Son and Spirit alongside the Father.

Tertullian illustrates this in *Praxeas* 8.5–7 by an image: Father, Son and Spirit are related to one another like a spring, river and canal, the canal being drawn from the river to irrigate the fields. Like the spring the Father is the inexhaustible origin of the deity; and just as the river rises from the spring, so the Son comes forth from the Father and brings salvation to human beings; and just as the water is distributed over the fields by canals, so the Holy Spirit is distributed to believers in baptism and makes them fruitful. It becomes clear here that there is only one divine substance – in the metaphor, the water; in reality Tertullian defines

divine substance as spirit (Latin *spiritus*), since John 4.24 says
'God is spirit.' The Father, the Son and the Holy Spirit are
spirit in substance. Consequently the word spirit can denote
two things in early Christianity, namely the Holy Spirit as
distinct from God the Father and God the Son, and also the
being, the substance of God, which is the same in all three
persons.

The illustration of the Trinity in terms of spring, river
and canal confirms the impression of a gradated order
that we know from contexts relating to the economy of
salvation. However, Tertullian attaches far more importance
to the precise understanding of this gradated order than
earlier schemes, since – already under pressure from the
Monarchian counter-position – he has to keep his theology
free from the suspicion that it is abandoning monotheism.
Therefore in *Praxeas* 9 he is concerned to make a precise
differentiation in trinitarian theological diction: for him,
while Father, Son and Spirit are different from one another
(*alius et alius et alius*), this differentiation must not be misin-
terpreted as radical difference (*diversitas*) in the sense of
division (*divisio*) or separation (*separatio*); on the other hand
it can be described as distribution (*distributio*), distinction
(*distinctio*) and articulated ordering (*dispositio*), so as to make
it possible at the same time to maintain the unity of the
divine persons.

Tertullian also uses the term person in respect of the
Trinity: the persons of the Godhead can be distinguished
with the help of 'prosopological exegesis', which asks of
each scriptural saying who the speaker (the *prosopon legon*)
of a particular verse is in the theological sense (cf. *Praxeas*
11). Tertullian demonstrates this, for example, by Ps. 110.1
(109.1 in the Septuagint); the verse runs: 'The Lord says to
my Lord: "Sit at my right hand ..."' In the church's interpretation the invitation itself is a saying of the Father to the
Son, but the verse as a whole – like all scriptural sayings – is
spoken by the Holy Spirit. In this way the scriptural sayings
'constitute' each person of the Trinity in its peculiarity. And
each person of the Trinity is given the title 'God' and 'Lord'
(thus *Praxeas* 13.6, 8), as is the Spirit – a clarification which

could not establish itself throughout the church until much later.

By comparison with Tertullian's reflection on the theology of the Trinity and its carefully balanced terminology, the Monarchian concept (despite a concern which can be understood) stands out as a simplistic solution to the problem discussed, though at the same time precisely because of its monotheistic focus it doubtless proved extremely attractive to believers. Tertullian himself concedes that the majority of believers, namely the simple people (*simplices*) whom he polemically denounces as uneducated and ignorant, are afraid of the concept of the *oikonomia* (which from their perspective stands suspiciously close to pagan polytheism) and then decisively insists on the *monarchia* of God (cf. *Praxeas* 3). And the most significant trinitarian theologian of the East, Origen, confirms in his discussion with Bishop Heraclides around 240 that believers would be offended if there were two Gods: therefore it must be shown how far both are two and how far they are one God (*Dialogue with Heraclides* 2). He says that much unrest has come about in the church over such questions, so that often writings have been presented which the bishops concerned and the perpetrators were to sign before all the people so that there should no longer be any unrest and no further investigation should take place (*Dialogue* 4). Accordingly the debate over Christian monotheism was not only a matter for professional theologians and community leaders but stirred people up over a wide area and over decades. While the Monarchian position broadly met with sympathy because of its clear confession of monotheism, it did not meet the standards of a biblical exegesis which in the meantime had become professional or the demands that trained theologians interested in philosophy thought should be made of the Christian image of God. Such theologians (e.g. Tertullian in the West and even more Origen in the East) had a lasting influence on the discussion through their teaching activity and their writings, and contributed towards forcing the Monarchian reading of monotheism on to the defensive.

However, the problem was not yet solved, for even such a brilliant thinker as Origen (died 253/4) did not succeed in summing up the unity and difference in God adequately. Origen was counted among the Logos theologians – no wonder, since he was probably the most educated Christian of his time; he had studied in Alexandria, the great cultural metropolis, and was versed not only in the biblical writings but also in pagan philosophy. For that reason he put forward a Logos theology which was grounded in both the Bible and philosophy, and made decisive attacks on the Monarchians.

Like the other Logos theologians, he was therefore more concerned to accentuate the distinction than the unity in God: Origen described Father, Son and Spirit as three distinct 'hypostases' (thus *Commentary on John* II 10.75). The Greek word *hypostasis* is derived from the verb *hyphistamai,* 'be present, exist', and in the philosophical context denotes an entity's real existence, its own reality. If Father, Son and Spirit are three hypostases, then they are three entities with their own existence and real presence, and their distinction is expressed.

However, Origen did not succeed in grasping the *unity* of the three conceptually. In his time it was not yet possible for Greek theologians to speak of the one divine nature (*physis*) or of the one divine substance (*ousia*). For the terms substance and hypostasis, *ousia* and *hypostasis*, were still interchangeable. Talk of three distinct hypostases could be interpreted to mean that each hypostasis has its own individual substance, its own *ousia*. Origen also shared this view, and he guarded against saying that Father and Son should be one in substance/*ousia* (cf. *Commentary on John* X 37.246); it was there that he recognized the Monarchian danger.

But how could Origen express the unity of Father, Son and Spirit? He designated these three as being one (*hen*) through harmony (*symphonia*) and identity of willing (thus *Against Celsus* VIII 12) – that is the usual approach of the Logos theologians, but it appears inadequate from our perspective, for the unity is to some degree a moral unity, not an essential one.

However, in Origen there is another starting point for the idea of an essential community between the three divine hypostases, since he attributes to the Father, the Son and the Spirit, in distinction from all other existing beings, the properties of immutability and essential goodness (cf. *On First Principles* I 8.3 and 6.2). All other existing beings are mutable, no other beings are good in themselves. However, if according to Origen the Father is unchangeably good and likewise the Son and the Spirit, then here there is something like a common property, a common 'nature'. But this is not conceptualized, and this terminological defect becomes evident in the dispute over Arianism, which broke out in Alexandria, the very place where Origen lived and taught for a long time.

Much later, after the conflict had been overcome and orthodoxy had established itself, Origen was criticized because his doctrine did not do justice to the new demands. This criticism was of course misguided, since even a great theologian such as Origen could not be ahead of his time and guess what orthodox christology and the doctrine of the Trinity would look like at the end of the fourth century. However, the delayed criticism led an ardent admirer of Origen, Rufinus of Aquileia, to improve his work. Around the year 400 Rufinus translated writings of Origen from Greek into Latin, including the important systematic work *On First Principles* (Greek *Peri archon/* Latin *De principiis*). In so doing he sometimes attributed falsely to his great model formulations which sounded orthodox at the end of the fourth century and were meant to protect Origen from contemporary criticism. In Rufinus's translation the common divine nature of Father, Son and Spirit then suddenly becomes a theme – here the original has been overpainted to make it orthodox, and it took many efforts by scholars to recognize the retouching as such and to rediscover the authentic Origen.

Origen's system is interesting in our context for yet another reason: deeply influenced by the Platonic view of the world, Origen expressed the opinion that all that is spiritual is eternal and only the material is transitory. Thus for him not only God the Father of the universe is eternal; his Son, the Logos, is also eternal, as is the Holy Spirit. And for Origen the other spiritual beings, the angels, the souls of human beings and the demons are also eternal. Here the great theologian expressed himself somewhat cautiously in order to give no offence. But he says clearly that God must always have been creator and ruler of all, otherwise he would have changed at creation and so to speak made progress; and to think that would be sheer blasphemy (cf. *Principles* I 2.10; toned down in I 4.3–5; but see also III 5.3f.).

By nature the spiritual beings (Origen calls them *logika*) were all equal to one another, and only through a pre-cosmic fall did the difference between angels, human souls and demons arise, depending on the severity of the sin. Because of this sin God created the material cosmos, so that the fallen spiritual beings would be caught in it, experience God's education and ultimately be redeemed by the Logos.

Here the question arises: if according to Origen *all* that is spiritual is eternal, what is the difference between the Logos as the Son of God and the other spiritual beings (*logika*)? At all events it is not that the spiritual beings, unlike the Logos, had a beginning at a particular time. Rather, the distinction consists in the particular relationship to God. The eternal Logos is begotten by the eternal Father as his image, but the spiritual beings have been created from eternity through the Logos and in him. That means that they have no direct relationship to God the Father as the highest principle, but only a mediated, indirect one. Therefore in the order of being they are clearly lower than the Logos, who is directly begotten by the Father.

All that sounds odd, and Origen's doctrine of the pre-existence of souls (or better spiritual beings) was firmly repudiated in the church. Possibly Origen suspected in advance that this could happen and therefore spoke only very cautiously of the eternity of the spiritual creation.

By contrast, his doctrine of the eternal begetting of the Logos (cf. *Principles* 2.2–4) had a greater influence: if according to Origen the Logos is begotten as Son by the Father and at the same time, like all that is spiritual, is eternal and always already with God, the begetting of the Son cannot be an event in time. In that case the Father had always been the Father of the Son (thus *Principles* I 2.2). And there was no time at which the Son was not (*Principles* I 2.9). Origen speaks explicitly of the eternal and everlasting begetting of the Son and compares it with the begetting of brightness by the light (thus *Principles* I 2.4). The brightness which a light begets immediately exists with this light and at the same time, and if one regards God the Father as eternal light, then the Son is the brightness which constantly and eternally goes out from the light.

Thus Origen – like the earlier Apologists and Logos theologians – distinguished between God the Father and the Logos begotten by him. He saw them as two really existing beings, as two hypostases. And to him, too, God the Logos appears lesser by comparison with God the Father, subordinate to him. But unlike the earlier Apologists Origen did not give any point in time for the emergence of the Logos from God, for the begetting of the Son. Most Apologists had seen this begetting in close connection with the creation of the world: in order to create the world God first brings forth his Logos, which puts God's will into action. The thought here is quite functional. But Origen presents the philosophical view of God more consistently than the Apologists before him: he knows that God never changes, and is immutable. Therefore the begetting of the Logos, too, cannot mean any change in God; it belongs to God the Father from eternity and cannot be thought of apart from him.

Origen made a pioneering contribution with this theory. The church may not have taken over his whole system, and after Origen's death it criticized and condemned him on some points. But the conviction that in the divine sphere there can be no measure of time, no before and after, and that the emergence of the Son and Spirit from the Father are not temporal events but eternal processes, became established in the long run, already in the dispute over Arianism.

But before we can turn to the occasion for this dispute, it is necessary briefly to mention some stages on the way there, though their concrete form and significance remain disputed.

In the time when Callistus was Bishop of Rome (*c.*217–22) Sabellius, an important representative of modalistic Monarchianism, was excommunicated there, although the official Roman theology of its time showed Monarchian tendencies (for which it was criticized by the dissident Hippolytus, who allowed himself to be appointed anti-bishop).

A generation later, in the middle of the third century (presumably around 262), there was a controversial exchange of letters on the doctrine of the Trinity between Bishop Dionysius of Alexandria and Bishop Dionysius of Rome: in it the Bishop of Alexandria, because he was facing modalistic Monarchians in neighbouring Libya, is said especially to have emphasized the threeness of the divine hypostases or the distinction of Father, Son and Spirit, whereas the Bishop of Rome protested against tearing apart the divine *monarchia*. It was important for him to emphasize the unity of God and he allegedly caused his fellow-bishop from Alexandria to modify his teaching in this direction. The problem here is that the content of this correspondence came to be known only a hundred years later, when the dispute over Arianism was in full swing. Therefore scholars today no longer rule out the possibility that parts of the correspondence were forged subsequently, in order to gain ammunition from it for the current conflict over Arius's theology. Possibly remarks were foisted on the two third-century bishops which were really made only in the fourth century. Various details are a matter of dispute.

It is the same with another theological discussion which is often counted as part of the prehistory of the dispute over Arianism: in the 260s (more precisely 264 and 268), the then Bishop of Antioch, Paul of Samosata, was criticized at synods for his christological views and finally deposed. Allegedly the concept of the consubstantiality of God the Father and the Son, the famous *homoousios*, was also condemned; as we know, it was to play a role at the Council of Nicaea in 325. Here too it should be noted that this report was circulated only in the course of the Arian dispute (*c.*358) – it is therefore quite probable that it was invented later in order to discredit the term *homoousios* and with it the whole Council of Nicaea. Today we can hardly reconstruct what Paul of Samosata really thought and taught because of the bad quality of the tradition.

We again find ourselves on somewhat firm ground when we attempt to depict the conflict over Arius of Alexandria.

CHAPTER 5

The Concern of Arius of Alexandria and the Reaction of his Opponents

Arius, who is said to have been born around 260, came from Libya and had a successful career as a presbyter in the church of Alexandria. The presbyters of this metropolis had a special status and were far from being limited to a representative function as the advisory council to the bishop. Some of them were in charge of the community of a whole area of the city, each with his own church, and consequently they bore a similar responsibility to the bishops of smaller cities. We may assume that these presbyters were correspondingly self-confident and did not always submit to their bishop without question.

This was also true of Arius. He was in charge of the community of part of Alexandria which met at the church of Baukalis. There Arius regularly presided at the eucharist, he preached and expounded the biblical writings. His reputation among colleagues and in his community was equally high, and there was no criticism of his lifestyle and his piety. If the tradition in Athanasius, *Oration against the Arians* I 5, is correct, he himself had a quite high opinion of his own education, which he said he had received from teachers who themselves 'had a portion of wisdom, had been instructed by God and were wise in all things'. However, we do not know who these teachers were. Scholars have long associated Arius with the presbyter and theologian Lucian of Antioch, who suffered martyrdom in 312, for in a letter on one occasion Arius speaks of a group of 'Syllucianists', among whom he numbers himself; this has been interpreted as a teacher-pupil relationship. In truth we know very little about Lucian of Antioch and have no idea whether Arius ever met him. The theology of Arius can be explained more from the Alexandrian milieu which was strongly shaped by the theology of Origen; we may presuppose that, like Origen before him, he had considerable sympathy for Hellenistic philosophy.

The dispute over Arius broke out around 318, or perhaps three or four years later. The occasion for it has been handed down to us only indirectly by a letter of the Emperor Constantine from the year 324 (the text has been preserved in Eusebius of Caesarea, *Life of Constantine* II 64–72). According to this, Bishop Alexander of Alexandria had required his presbyters to state their views on a difficult passage of the Old Testament. What Arius, who at that time was probably already close to his sixties, said displeased the bishop and led him to take proceedings against Arius and his friends. Unfortunately the emperor's letter does not indicate what the Old Testament passage was. However, from the further course of the dispute we can conjecture that it was the eighth chapter of the book of Proverbs, which Christians read in the Greek translation of the Septuagint (LXX). In this chapter personified Wisdom appears, who according to the Old Testament wisdom tradition was God's helper at creation, but who in the early church was predominantly interpreted as the Son of God, the Logos, by whom all things were made, as John 1.3 states.

In Prov. 8.22–25 the following words are put in the mouth of Wisdom/the Logos: 'The Lord created me as the beginning of his ways to his works. Before the Age (Greek *aion*) he set me up, in the beginning, before he made the earth and the depths, before the springs abounding water came forth. Before the mountains had been shaped, before all the hills, he begets me.' If we refer these words to the Son of God, the Logos, according to scripture he was 'created – set up – begotten': but how is that to be interpreted? Arius inferred from the text that the Son of God, the Logos, had a *beginning* – certainly before the earth, the depths, the springs, before the mountains and hills and even before the time of the world (*aion*); but he did have a beginning, and for this beginning of the Logos scripture uses not only the metaphor 'begetting' (which is common in the church) but also the term 'creation'.

With his exegesis Arius was pursuing a particular concern: he believed that here he had found the key to the old problem of how christology could be reconciled with monotheism, belief in the one and only God: if the pre-existent Son of God had a beginning, then he did not exist before he was 'begotten, created and set up'. Before the 'begetting, creating or setting up' of the Son, God existed alone. This sole eternal God is the only true God; he was not always 'the Father', but became the Father through the 'begetting, creating and setting up' of the Son.

Behind this stands a deepened reflection on the concept of God. What really marks God out as God, what distinguishes him from all other beings? For Arius the answer was: everything that is not God in the real sense has a cause or a beginning (the Greek word *arche* means both; it does not just indicate the beginning of existence but also has connotations of causality). The only true God is alone *anarchos*, for him no *arche*, cause or even beginning, can be indicated; he exists eternally from himself, absolute, and thus is the last and only principle of all being.

By contrast, the pre-existent Son of God, the Logos, is – as the whole church clearly teaches – 'begotten' by the Father: he has an *arche*, a cause, and for Arius thus also a beginning. In Prov. 8.22–25 scripture describes the origin or coming into being of the Logos as 'begetting, creating, setting up' by God. But this origin clearly distinguishes the Logos from the God without origin and therefore the Logos cannot be 'true God'; by nature he is other than the only true God, in that he came into being. By making the concept of God precise in this way, the problem of Christian monotheism is solved: God in the real sense is only one, namely the God without origin.

For Arius, the Son of God, the Logos, belongs on another level of being than the only true God, the Father. Moreover, he does not explain the origin of the Logos as the early Apologists (for example Justin) do, in connection with Stoic philosophy, to the effect that the Father has expressed his own inner Logos (the *logos endiathetos*) or his wisdom, that he has 'spoken' his Word and thus given it its own existence (as *logos prophorikos*). For Arius, the Son of God is not God's *inner* Logos, God's *own* reason and wisdom, which gains independent existence through the process of 'begetting'; the Son came into being out of nothing as God's image, by the *will* of God. Precisely because he is God's image, he is also called Logos and Wisdom, and one may even call him God, but all these designations are not used in the real sense. The Son of God is not 'true' God; he only bears the title God. Nor is he unchangeably good like the true God; he is by nature mutable and is steadfast in the good only by virtue of his own free will. Ontologically the Son belongs more on the side of the creatures, all of whom have also come into being out of nothing. However, by comparison with the other creatures the Son of God occupies a special position, for they are all created through him (according to John 1.3); he is the mediator at creation, whereas in his own begetting or creation there is no mediator of creation.

Arius concluded from Prov. 8.22 that the pre-existent 'divine' Logos is a creature of the only true God. His doctrine focused and radicalized the older Logos theology and heightened the element of subordination that had already been inherent in this theology at an earlier stage by giving an ontological explanation of the subordination in the economy of salvation: God the Father and Son belong to different levels of being; despite his special position as mediator of creation, the Logos is ontologically closer to the (other) creatures than he is to the Father; he is so radically subordinate to the Father that in Arius's view he cannot even know the nature of the Father. Thus christology no longer represents a threat to monotheism, since it does not touch the level of the true Godhead at all. The Logos offers no competition to the only true God, for he is not God in the real sense, but a unique creature.

For many Christian contemporaries the great provocation was that Arius defined the 'God Logos' of whom the church spoke as a 'creature'. One of those provoked was Alexander, Bishop of Alexandria, who argued against Arius that God the Father was *always* the Father because the Son *always* existed. For Bishop Alexander the Son is in truth *God's* Logos and *God's* wisdom and therefore also *in his being* the Son of God; he is begotten *of the Father* – not from nothing! – and his divinity is quite indisputable. Alexander regarded Arius's teaching as an attack on the divinity of Christ; consequently he saw the long-serving presbyter as fighting against Christ, as a heretic against whom action had to be taken.

Probably around 318 or 319 Arius and his supporters were deposed and excommunicated. They formed a group of seven presbyters and twelve deacons, who had been joined by two bishops from small places in Libya. However, because they felt that they were completely in the right, they did not submit to this judgement but went off to Palestine to seek allies there. Arius found support from Eusebius, the Bishop of Nicomedia, the imperial residence in Asia Minor, a skilful church politician who was already corresponding with him, and also from the bishop and church historian Eusebius of Caesarea Maritima in Palestine.

Encouraged by the support of these important bishops, around 320 Arius and his followers again wrote to their home bishop (Document 6 in Opitz, *Urkunden*, see Bibliography) in order once again to present their own teaching, to justify it and to distinguish it from any heresy that was universally condemned. Arius wrote:

> We know one God, who as the only one is unbegotten, as the only one is eternal, as the only one is without beginning/cause (Greek *anarchos*), as the only one is true (God) ... immutable and unchangeable ... before eternal times he begot the only-begotten Son ... he did not beget him by appearance but in truth, by calling him into being

by his own will ... as the perfect creature of God – but not
as one of the (other) creatures ... he is not an emanation
as (the Gnostic) Valentinus taught, nor is he a part of the
Father of the same substance (*homoousion meros*), as (the
Persian) Mani declared ... Nor (do we believe) that he
who already was was begotten or created later as Son; you
yourself, holy father (*papa*), have constantly reprimanded
in church and in the assembly those who introduce such
a thing ... Thus there are three hypostases. God, in so far
as he is the author of all, is the most only one [*sic*] without
beginning/cause (*anarchos*); the Son was begotten by the
Father outside time and created and set up (cf. Prov.
8.22–25) before the ages; he was not there before he was
begotten ... and came into being as the only one by the
Father. Nor is he eternal or co-eternal with the Father or
equally unbegotten, and he does not possess being at the
same time with the Father, as some claim, introducing
two unbegotten principles of origin (*archai*) ... Now if
the word of scripture ... 'I came forth from the Father
and have come ...' (John 16.28) is understood by some
to mean that (the Son) is part of him (viz. God) who is
of the same substance ... the Father would be composite,
divisible, changeable and a body ...

In his remarks Arius seeks to demonstrate agreement with
Bishop Alexander, making a common front against the
paradoxical Monarchian doctrine (according to which the
Father himself is begotten as Son), but at the same time
he wants to demonstrate his own conception plausibly:
there cannot be *two* equally eternal principles, otherwise
monotheism would be at risk. Nor can the Son be a part
of the Father and of the same substance – at this point
the adjective *homoousios*, which later became so famous,
comes into play and is rejected by Arius as an element of
Manichaean heresy; however, here the point is that it would
be unseemly to assume that God was divisible like a body
– the Son cannot be a 'part' of the Father! Thus in Arius's
view only one solution remains, which he supports with
a reference to Prov. 8.22–25: the Son must be an extraor-
dinary creature, the only creature which has been 'begotten,

created and set up' solely by the Father, but he is a caused being, and does not put in question the uniqueness of the true God, who knows no cause.

The bishops of Nicomedia and Caesarea also supported Arius's teaching in letters. They emphasized that there could not be two principles without origin and that therefore the Son must have had a beginning. That also convinced some bishops in Palestine, Syria and Asia Minor. Probably around 320, synods were held in the province of Bithynia in Asia Minor and in Palestine under the leadership of Eusebius of Nicomedia or Eusebius of Caesarea which rehabilitated Arius and called for him to be taken back into the church of Alexandria.

On the other side Bishop Alexander of Alexandria wrote encyclicals to his fellow bishops in which he warned them against the intrigues of Arius and his followers. It was certainly also important here that Alexander felt that the support of outside bishops for the Alexandrian presbyter Arius amounted to meddling in the affairs of his church which contradicted the rules of *communio*, church fellowship. The Bishop of Alexandria also attempted to counter the substance of Arius's argument: in his letter (cf. Document 14 in Opitz, *Urkunden*) he emphasized that the Father alone is unbegotten, that the Father remains the same for ever and knows neither progress nor diminution. This is directed against the assumption that God becomes the Father only at a later stage and in so doing has become 'more' than he was before or has suffered a loss in his being by begetting the Son. For Alexander, the Son of God is not begotten out of that which is not, but from the Father who is, in an ineffable and inexpressible way which no one can grasp. Arius's rationalist explanation that the 'begetting' of the Son amounts to creation out of nothing by the will of the Father is thus rejected; Alexander also counters the Arian doctrine that the Son has a beginning by saying that the Son is always already from the Father and that his begetting is without beginning (Greek *anarchos*), but that the eternal being of the Son does not amount to his being unbegotten, for this is the one distinctive characteristic which the Father has: indeed the Saviour himself says, 'The Father is greater than I' (John 14.28).

If we compare the texts of the adversaries, the logical stringency of the Arian conception (which convinced Arius's sympathizers) is striking, whereas Alexander seems to be manoeuvring: he says that the Son is eternal but not unbegotten, though no one can explain his 'begetting'. That seems clumsy, almost an evasion, although the point of the argument is clear: Alexander does not understand the metaphor of 'begetting' as the cipher for a quasi-temporal beginning but as the description of an eternal causality; and he wants to maintain the true divinity of the saviour – a soteriological motive which was to take on decisive significance in this dispute.

The dispute spread and the fronts hardened. This was the point in time at which Emperor Constantine intervened in the conflict.

CHAPTER 6

The Intervention of Emperor Constantine and the Council of Nicaea

In 324 Constantine had defeated Licinius, his last rival for sole rule of the Roman Empire, and thus also brought the eastern half of the empire (in which the dispute over Arius was raging) under his control. At this point Constantine's sympathy for Christianity had already become clear; nevertheless, the emperor was rooted in the Roman understanding of religion in so far as he regarded Christianity primarily as a cult religion whose task it was to safeguard the favour of the deity through prayers and cultic celebrations. Thus Christianity had been given the function of supporting the state, because the prosperity of the empire and the successful rule of the emperor depended on the practice of Christian worship free from disruption. Constantine was determined to guarantee precisely this.

After taking power in the East the emperor saw himself confronted with the dispute over Arius. The lack of unity among Christians alarmed Constantine, since it affected the foundations of his religious views: if the benevolence of the deity was dependent on Christians worshipping God rightly, any lack of unity and any division could only have negative effects. It was not the subject-matter of the conflict that brought Constantine on the scene, but the very fact of division.

That can be read in a letter which Emperor Constantine wrote in 324 to the protagonists in the dispute, Bishop Alexander and the presbyter Arius (handed down in Eusebius, *Life of Constantine* II 64–72). In it the emperor completely plays down the substance of the conflict by describing it as a trifle, an insignificant difference of opinion on doctrinal questions, of the kind that can also occur, say, in a philosophical school without the whole school having to split and collapse as a result. He says that the main point is agreement in essentials (i.e. in the Christian faith and the right worship of God); this agreement must not be put in question by such trivia, namely the discussion of a biblical passage that should never have been made public. Therefore the opponents are immediately to bury their differences of opinion, be reconciled and return to the former harmony.

Church historians have condemned Constantine's letter as a completely wrong assessment of the true situation. The monarch, who had not yet even been baptized, evidently had no deeper understanding of the explosiveness of the heated debate over Christian monotheism. His perspective was that of a Roman emperor who wanted to promote the unity of religion in order to ensure for himself the protection of the supreme deity. His intervention in the dispute over Arius was no exception here. In other conflicts, too, the emperor made efforts to restore church unity, as in the Donatist schism in North Africa, the Melitian schism in Egypt, and the Novatian schism, which had adherents not only in Rome but also in the East. Indeed, Constantine did not even want to allow Easter to be celebrated on two different dates: he aimed at a single Easter festival. The unity of the cult, the unity of the church, the prosperity of the state and the success of imperial policy through the favour of the deity are the guidelines of the church-political programme which Constantine also pursued in his letter to Bishop Alexander and Arius.

Constantine had this letter delivered by a Spanish bishop, Ossius of Cordoba, who had been in the emperor's entourage for some time and had gained influence over him. This bishop was probably not a particularly outstanding theologian, otherwise he would not have undertaken such a hopeless attempt at mediation. For the attempt at reconciliation failed totally – neither Arius nor Bishop Alexander was prepared to depart from his standpoint. Nor was the dispute only over theology; it was also about the question of church discipline. Alexander, whose episcopal authority had been put in question by Arius and his friends, certainly did not want to suffer any further loss of face. And conversely the presbyter Arius was so strengthened by the support that he had found in the meantime that there was no longer any question of his yielding.

Ossius had to return without having achieved anything. On the way, at the beginning of 325, he took part in a synod in Syrian Antioch, the third largest metropolis of the empire, which had met to elect a new bishop. Bishop Eusebius from neighbouring Caesarea at Palestine, who had supported Arius, was also at this episcopal election. However, an opponent of Arius and declared friend of Alexander of Alexandria, Eustathius from Beroea, was elected. So the majority at the synod were unfavourable to Arius's cause and of course also to Bishop Eusebius of Caesarea; moreover this is documented in the synod's letter (cf. Document 18 in Opitz, *Urkunden*), which goes into the dispute over Arius. The assembled bishops composed a creed which contradicted Arius's key theses: according to it the Son is begotten *from the Father* and did not come into being from nothing, even though no one can describe his begetting. He has always existed; however, he is not unbegotten but – according to the biblical writings – Son begotten in truth and in the real sense, and also unchangeable and unalterable in his being. All but three bishops at the synod (one of whom was Eusebius of Caesarea) agreed in this view. These three bishops were denied *communio*, as had become customary in the more serious disputes in the church.

What was unusual, however, was the announcement that the three bishops mentioned would be given another occasion to justify themselves at a future major synod.

We may assume that account was taken of the emperor's wish for union and harmony in the church on this point. Originally Ancyra, present-day Ankara in central Anatolia, was envisaged for this synod, but for practical reasons it was then held in the imperial summer residence in Nicaea in Asia Minor.

The organization and logistics of the whole enterprise lay in the hands of the emperor, who had really planned this episcopal assembly as an 'ecumenical' synod, i.e. as a synod of the whole empire. However, despite Constantine's efforts the number of Western participants remained low. Bishop Sylvester of Rome refused to take part in the synod, pleading his advanced age, and instead sent two legates, the presbyters Vitus and Vincentius, who were to play a role in the further course of the Arian dispute. Most of the bishops who travelled there – in number more than 250 – came from the eastern provinces of the empire, from Egypt, Palestine, Syria, Asia Minor and Mesopotamia, but also from Greece and the Balkans. Individual bishops travelled from beyond the frontiers of the empire (from Persia, the Caucasus and Gothic territories).

In June 325 the deliberations began; they were held in Greek, as the whole theological dispute over Arius so far had been. Only at first glance might this seem to be an incidental matter. For in the years and decades after Nicaea it was to prove that the church in the West, which had been using Latin as a theological language for just under a century, could not always follow the finer details of the Greek discussion, with the result that because of the difference in language people sometimes missed the point.

No acts of the council have been preserved, only reports from participants, which of course were necessarily partisan. Eusebius of Caesarea describes the solemn entry of the emperor into the hall; he mentions that there were welcoming addresses and that the emperor himself intervened in the negotiations and made repeated calls for harmony. As had been provided for at the previous synod of Antioch, Eusebius was offered the opportunity to justify himself with a creed (Greek *symbolon*) in the presence of the emperor.

It had already become customary in the dispute over Arius for the opposing parties to sum up their theological views in creeds. If we compare these creeds, we recognize that they are constructed according to the same principles and are similar in structure. Here research speaks quite vividly of a 'building-block system', for as a rule the confessions consist of three basic building blocks, namely belief in God the Father, the Son and the Holy Spirit. The building blocks can be further differentiated, the passage about christology being of particular interest in the Arian dispute. This passage in turn is composed of two parts: the first part (over which there was special dispute) is concerned with the pre-existence of the Saviour, the second with his incarnation.

Eusebius now introduced his own creed (see Document 22 in Opitz, *Urkunden*) into the debate with great skill by anchoring it in the tradition of his home church:

> As we have received from the bishops who preceded us, and in our first catechizings, and when we received baptism, and as we have learned from the divine scriptures, and as we constantly believed and taught as presbyter and bishop, so believing also at the time present, we report to you our faith, and it is this:
>
> 'We believe in One God Father, Almighty, the Maker of all things visible and invisible. And in One Lord Jesus Christ, the Logos of God, God from God, Light from Light, Life from Life, Only-begotten Son, firstborn of all creation, before all ages begotten from the Father, by Whom also all things were made; Who for our salvation was incarnate, and lived among men, and suffered, and rose again the third day, and ascended to the Father, and will come again in glory to judge living and dead. And we believe also in One Holy Spirit. We believe that each of these is and exists, the Father truly Father, the Son truly Son, the Holy Spirit truly Holy Spirit; thus also our Lord said sending out his disciples for preaching: "Go and teach all nations baptizing them in the name of the Father and the Son and the Holy Spirit" (Matt. 28.19).'

The statements of the creed on christological pre-existence seem acceptable to the church as a whole; they have a biblical foundation and are carefully balanced: Christ is the 'only-begotten Son' – thus a reading of John 1.18 which appears in some ancient manuscripts (at this point others read: he is the only-begotten God). But alongside this designation from the Gospel of John the creed immediately puts another from the letter to the Colossians: Christ is the 'firstborn of all creation' (1.15). This formulation seems to meet with Arius's ideas, because it puts Christ so to speak at the head of the creatures, but is also backed by the authority of the New Testament. Eusebius, who was a wise man and could think dialectically, had a reason for putting the two christo-logical titles from the Gospel of John and the letter to the Colossians side by side: from the perspective of the Father Christ is the only-begotten Son, from the side of creatures he is the firstborn of all creation. So he occupies precisely that position as mediator which the Logos theology of the Apologists had always assigned to him.

In addition, in an explanation of the confession of Father, Son and Spirit, the Bishop of Caesarea makes it clear that each of the three really exists, and as a basis for his view refers to the command of the risen Christ to baptize in Matt. 28.19. This clarification is not just a matter of course, as might seem at first sight. Rather, it makes a point against any Monarchian theology. For Eusebius wants to maintain that the distinction between Father, Son and Spirit is real and not just nominal. In their own existence Father, Son and Spirit are three and not just one. In substance here we have Origen's concept of hypostasis, even if Eusebius does not use it directly. However, the Bishop of Caesarea stands clearly in the tradition of Origen: like Origen he is a Logos theologian and therefore an opponent of Monarchian christ-ology.

With this creed Eusebius was completely in line with the emperor's aim of presenting a result acceptable to all sides. And the Bishop of Caesarea could proudly report to the members of his community that the creed had not only been read out in the emperor's presence but had been found right and good. The emperor had been the first to express this view.

Nevertheless there was a catch here. The statements of the creed remained ambiguous – even Arius could have subscribed to them (if need be): however, he would have had to interpret them, say, to mean that while Jesus Christ is 'God's Logos', he is not so in the real sense, and while he is likewise 'God from God' he is not *true* God' like the Father. Arius could also have endorsed the begetting of the Son from the Father before all ages by saying that 'begetting from the Father' meant 'creation by the will of the Father' and that the Son had a beginning 'before all ages'. The radical core statements of Arian doctrine (which speak of the non-existence of the Son before the begetting, his creation out of nothing and his mutability) may not have been repeated in Eusebius's creed, but the creed did not refute them. That was the problem, since the majority of council fathers evidently wanted a clearer stand against the provocations of Arius. Therefore a new creed had to be worked out, the famous Nicene Creed.

Scholars used to trust Eusebius's information that his own confession served as the basis for the Nicene Creed and that only a few additions were made. However, doubts soon arose about this account, for of course Eusebius is clearly concerned to put his own role at the council in the most favourable possible light for his community in Caesarea. For some time another traditional creed was then sought which would have been revised at Nicaea. However, it is now assumed that the Nicene Creed, too, was constructed on the 'building-block' principle. In other words, the council fathers, or perhaps better a council commission which was to work out the creed, chose those theological 'building blocks' from earlier creeds which were undisputed and reformulated those at issue in the Arian dispute, namely the statements about the pre-existence of the saviour. The result of this work (see Document 24 in Opitz, *Urkunden*) was as follows:

> We believe in One God Father, Almighty, the Maker of all things visible and invisible. And in One Lord Jesus Christ,

the Son of God, begotten from the Father, Only-begotten, that is from the substance of the Father; God from God, Light from Light, true God from true God, begotten not made, consubstantial with the Father, by whom all things were made, both things in heaven and things on earth; who for us men and for our salvation came down and was incarnate, was made man, suffered, and rose again the third day, ascended into heaven, and is coming to judge living and dead. And in the Holy Spirit.

And those who say 'There once was when He was not' and 'Before being begotten He was not,' and 'He came into being out of nothing,' or those who pretend that the Son of God is 'from another hypostasis or substance', or 'created', or 'alterable', or 'mutable', the Catholic and Apostolic Church anathematizes.

Those familiar with the material will recognize the clarifications in the christological passages of the creed: it is stated that the only-begotten Son is begotten *'from the substance* (Greek *ousia*) of the Father' – this addition bars the way to the Arian interpretation of the metaphor of begetting, for it means that the Son derives from the (divine) substance of the Father and has the same basis of being as the Father. Arius vigorously contested this particular theory, because in his view its consequence was that the Son was as equally without origin as the Father, and that would endanger monotheism.

The statement that Jesus Christ is *'true* God from true God' is also anti-Arian. Here we do not have an additional rhetorical cliché which has been inserted into the creed; rather, the core of Arian doctrine is affected, namely that the Son can be called God only in an honorary way, but is not *true God* (in the ontological sense) as the Father is. By contrast, for the majority of the council the divinity of Jesus Christ is no mere honour bestowed on the Son by grace, but is in full accord with reality. This has consequences for soteriology, since in Arius's system a (perfect) creature redeems the other creatures; the council fathers differ, seeing redemption guaranteed by the true divinity of the saviour.

To emphasize that once again it is also said that the Son is 'begotten, not made'. Arius had taught that the 'begetting' of the Son was to be understood as 'creation out of nothing'. Not so the Council of Nicaea. The only appropriate term for the origin of the Son from the Father is here the metaphor of begetting; the interpretation that the Son is made (in the sense of created) like the other creatures is excluded.

The next phrase, the statement that the Son is 'consubstantial', i.e. of the same substance or of one substance with the Father (Greek *homoousios to patri*), is regarded as the core statement of the creed of Nicaea, though it is only one of several anti-Arian points and is not even the clearest. Simply trying to translate the adjective shows the difficulty of interpretation. Is it stated that the substance (the *ousia*) of the Son is identical with the substance (*ousia*) of the Father? Thought through radically, that could mean that the Son is identical with the Father – that would be the Monarchian solution, which was completely unacceptable to theologians from Origen's tradition. But one could also interpret the adjective in another way, namely that the substance of the Son is completely equal to the substance of the Father; thus both the Father's and the Son's own existence would be kept, indeed one could even distinguish numerically the substance (the *ousia*) of the Son from the substance (the *ousia*) of the Father, although the two are completely equal. Bishops such as Eusebius of Caesarea, who subscribed to the creed of Nicaea with many reservations, preferred this view. The council itself did not explain the meaning of the adjective *homoousios*, and that was to provoke many more discussions.

It is also unclear on whose initiative this formulation really found its way into the text of the creed. The different traditions, that the emperor himself or his advisor from the West, Ossius of Cordoba, are responsible for it, have not proved convincing. Possibly the adjective was even thrown into the debate by a friend of Arius in order to show his opponents the horrific consequences of their theology – indeed, some years earlier Arius had already engaged in polemic against the 'Manichaean' heresy that the Son is a 'part' of the Father 'of the same substance'. However, if it became clear to the council fathers that the term *homoousios* was intolerable to the Arians, the bishops would have accepted the adjective into the council text without further ado. Be this as it may, the term *homoousios* belongs in the anti-Arian repertoire of the Council of Nicaea. Whereas today we associate the Nicene Creed with this word, at the time it by no means played *the* central role. It took almost thirty years for the term to be brought back into the foreground in the theological discussion.

However, the council fathers did not content themselves with an affirmative creed; they also condemned the core theses of Arius, which are listed in the appendix, including the assertion that the Logos/Son had 'once' not existed (Arius had carefully avoided the terms 'time' or 'aeon' in this context); the statement that the Son of God came into being out of nothing, from another hypostasis or another substance (*ousia*), is also rejected, in order indirectly to confirm that the Son derives from the hypostasis and the substance (the *ousia*) of the Father. At the same time, however, the formulation shows that the council fathers used the terms hypostasis and substance (*ousia*) as synonyms and did not distinguish them. This was to pose a problem in the future.

The whole text was put to the vote by the assembly of bishops in June 325. The discussions had shown that the majority of the bishops stood behind the text. Thus the emperor's aim, church unity, seemed to have been brought within reach. When it then turned out that a small minority of around twenty bishops would refuse their assent, Constantine reacted sharply. He threatened the bishops concerned with immediate banishment. With this threat he demonstrated that he was not willing to risk the failure of his religious policy because of the scruples of individual bishops. The driving motive here was not simply a personal lust for rule – although Constantine was very much a power-politician – but the typical Roman understanding of his role as emperor, with the ultimate responsibility for maintaining the unity of the cult that supported the state. Here the influence of politics on the church and on theological development emerged clearly. From then on, forcible political measures such as deposing and exiling recalcitrant bishops became part of church reality. In view of this development, even those who promoted the resolutions of the synod of Nicaea were uneasy.

The majority of opposing bishops allowed themselves to be intimidated by Constantine or sought to act tactically; the opposition melted away. However, Arius himself, together with the two Libyan bishops who had supported him from the beginning, resisted imperial pressure. They were banished from their homeland of Egypt. Nor did Bishop Eusebius of Nicomedia and the local bishop of Nicaea submit unconditionally. They signed the creed but not the anathemas (condemnations) of the council and thus refused to reject the core Arian statements. Constantine granted them some time for reflection. Instead of giving way, at this point Eusebius again showed solidarity with Arius and was promptly sent into exile in Gaul by the emperor, along with his fellow-bishop of Nicaea.

Constantine seemed to have achieved his aims: the Council of Nicaea – his council! – had restored church unity by resolving the doctrinal dispute through the decision of an overwhelming majority of bishops. Granted, in the end the emperor had exerted great pressure, but to him that probably did not seem inappropriate, merely consistent. In the end the number of 'victims' proved few – Constantine might be content, all the more so since other points of dispute within the church had also been removed: they need not concern us further here.

However, it was soon to prove that the dispute over the doctrine of the Trinity had by no means been settled with the council.

CHAPTER 7

The Development in the Period after the Council

The Council of Nicaea seemed to have restored the theological consensus and thus church peace. However, initially the consequences of its creed remained few. There had (largely) been agreement only on the repudiation of Arius's radical theses, and this result proved lasting. On the other hand, there continued to be dispute over the real core question of the theology of the Trinity: are Father, Son and Spirit three distinct entities or only one? The Council of Nicaea had not answered this question; the official harmony concealed the theological differences which were present and which fuelled new discussions and disputes.

In addition, the Emperor Constantine, who in 326 had celebrated the twentieth anniversary of his accession in the old imperial capital Rome, apparently performed a complete U-turn in his religious policy after his return to the East. Banished dignitaries such as Arius and Bishop Eusebius of Nicomedia were rehabilitated, while at the same time Nicene bishops were deposed and sent into exile – an amazing development. In truth Constantine did not in any way change the basic principles of his policy. The unity of the Christian church still remained the supreme norm for his action. He did not put the Council of Nicaea in question and the Nicene Creed was in no way taken back! Rather,

Constantine showed himself concerned to reintegrate the opponents of the council into the church and thus to crown his work of peace. The emperor was still unwilling to allow the church peace to be disturbed, even if the supposed disturbers of the peace came from the Nicene camp.

Nor did the rehabilitation of Arius and his friends mean that the emperor turned towards Arianism; conditions were attached. The Arian theologians had to adhere formally to the official church peace. Arius made a beginning here together with the deacon Euzoius, who would still be playing a role 30 years later as Bishop of Antioch. At the emperor's invitation they sent him a written creed from their exile in Illyrium (see Document 30 in Opitz, *Urkunden*), which was to document their agreement with the church's faith. Here again the statements about christological pre-existence attached to the confession of the one God are the decisive feature:

> We believe in one God Father, the Almighty, and in the Lord Jesus Christ, his Son, the only-begotten, who has been begotten from him before all ages, the God Logos, by whom all things were made, both things in heavens and things on earth ...

How are these statements to be interpreted? As a resolute change of direction by Arius, as a recanting of his convictions and a gesture of submission? The creed presented in no way hits the point of the Nicene Creed. It lacks the precise anti-Arian statements – for example that the Son is *true* God, begotten *from the substance* of the Father and *of the same substance* as him, that he is begotten and *not made*. Certainly Arius deliberately avoided these statements so as not to give up his own theology completely. The text is most similar to the creed which Eusebius of Caesarea had presented in the council (and which Arius himself could have adopted if need be) – the council found this creed, too, to 'be good and right'. Along these lines a welcome way out was offered to Arius, for of course he had to guard against repeating the core theses of his which had been condemned. So (in some respects) he followed Eusebius's example and like him referred in the appendix to his creed to the baptismal command of the risen Christ in Matt. 28.19 in order to indicate at least cryptically the real difference between Father, Son and Spirit.

The conclusion to the letter was also shaped so as totally to meet with the emperor's wishes: Arius and his fellow bishops asked again to be united with the church, since now the disputed questions and the superfluous chatter over these problems were ended. They said that it was their aim to keep peace with the church and to be able to offer the customary prayers for the peaceful and pious rule of Constantine – one might almost think that the emperor himself had inspired these lines. We may at least say that in the meantime the authors of the letter had acclimatized themselves to the way that the emperor thought. And their tactics were successful.

Constantine supported the reinstatement of the presbyter in his home community of Alexandria but came up against resistance there. Bishop Alexander had died in 328 and his successor Athanasius remained completely deaf to the repeated urgings of the emperor (who was already threatening him with deposition and exile): one could hardly claim that he gained the particular sympathy of Constantine with this stubbornness. Despite the imperial initiative, Arius could not return to Alexandria; his fate remained in the balance until he was finally rehabilitated (after the deposition of Athanasius in 335). However, the old man himself derived no advantage from this, since he died shortly after he had received news of the positive turn in events.

In these years Arius, who had increasingly become a marginal figure in history, no longer had any influence on theological developments. Now other theologians and church politicians in the east of the empire took up the baton. Here a significant role was played by the two bishops Eusebius of Caesarea and Eusebius of Nicomedia. The latter had been banished to Gaul after the Council of Nicaea because he had been unwilling to condemn Arius directly. Now, in connection with the emperor's efforts to reintegrate

Arius, he too succeeded in gaining permission to return to his episcopal see of Nicomedia.

Neither bishop was content with the result of the Council of Nicaea. Though their theological views were less extreme than those of Arius, they thought that the Nicene Creed had not struck the right balance. On the basis of their experiences with Constantine, however, the two bishops were clear that direct opposition to the imperial council was senseless or dangerous. So they sought to achieve success in another way. In the years after Nicaea, in the east of the empire a witch-hunt against Nicene bishops began. It always followed the same pattern: the bishops concerned (such as Eustathius of Antioch) were accused one by one, so that it did not look as if this was a theological dispute which could endanger church peace, but as if there were only individual cases. And of course these bishops were not accused in connection with the Nicene faith – the emperor would never have allowed that. Instead, charges were fabricated relating to church morality and discipline, on the basis of which each one of the bishops was condemned and deposed by a regional synod.

This procedure was also used against Bishop Athanasius of Alexandria, but over the years he vigorously defended himself and was time and again able to prevent his condemnation until he was finally deposed by a synod in Tyre in 335 for 'sacrilege'. A last desperate appeal to the emperor in Constantinople was of no avail – Athanasius was banished to Trier.

Thus the strategy of the Eusebians proved successful, although (or better, precisely because) theological questions were left aside. However, the different case of Bishop Marcellus of Ancyra proved to be an exception. Marcellus, who must have been born around 280, had to watch friendly fellow-bishops gradually being removed from their sees after the Council of Nicaea (the result of which completely accorded with his wishes). He certainly suspected that one day he too would become one of them. And he was clear-sighted enough to recognize that all these processes against Nicene bishops were not in fact about disciplinary questions but were introduced in order to make the Council of Nicaea in some way ineffective after the event.

Marcellus assumed that the wool was being pulled over the emperor's eyes by the Eusebians and that Constantine did not perceive how 'his' council and creed was gradually being undermined. Therefore the Bishop of Ancyra resolved not simply to wait quietly, but to move the dispute back to the theological field where it truly belonged. In 336, immediately after the banishment of Athanasius, he wrote a work on christology which he dedicated to the emperor himself and personally delivered to Constantine with a request for his verdict on it. Evidently he was convinced that he was advocating the very christology that would find the emperor's approval because it corresponded with the Nicene faith. So at the same time Marcellus took the opportunity to blacken his opponents to the emperor for their false theology and thus bring about a shift in the emperor's policy on religion.

He proved to have miscalculated badly. His considerations were based on a false assessment. The emperor was not so much concerned with the Nicene doctrine as such as with a theological basis on which the unity of the church could be guaranteed. In 335, in Constantine's view, peace seemed finally to have been restored, so when in this situation an individual bishop such as Marcellus attempted to get discussion going again, he was inevitably endangering the emperor's work of reunion, especially since of course contrary voices immediately made themselves heard. At the end of 336 a synod met in Constantinople which condemned Marcellus's book and brought about his deposition. On the orders of the emperor Marcellus went into exile.

If we look more closely at Marcellus's original theology we can understand why he provoked such energetic resistance from the Eusebians and became the bogey-man of the majority party in the East; at the same time we can understand why the Nicene Creed was discredited for many years, since Marcellus was one of its most ardent champions!

Looking at it from a greater distance, we can say that Marcellus's theology represented a new version of the Monarchian concern, but in a different form and at a more demanding intellectual and biblical level. Like the Monarchians at the beginning of the third century, Marcellus's central concern was the unity of God, or more precisely a demonstration that the creator God of the Old Testament and the saviour are not two Gods but one and the same God.

Marcellus expressed the oneness of God with many terms: he called God a *monas*, i.e. a unity, he spoke of the one divine *ousia* (the one divine substance) and the one divine hypostasis. In so doing he deliberately opposed his christology to the tradition of Origen, which continued to have an influence among theologians such as Eusebius of Caesarea: Origen had spoken emphatically of Father, Son and Spirit as *three* distinct hypostases, i.e. *three* distinct entities, whose real existence was to be maintained. Marcellus wanted to contradict precisely this. Only the one God has a real existence of his own, so there is also only *one* hypostasis and *one* divine substance. Marcellus went so far as also to speak of the *one* divine *prosopon*, the one divine person, and here at the latest agreement with most theologians in the East was completely illusory.

Marcellus engaged in polemic against Origen's three-hypostases doctrine, which he charged with being too close to Platonic philosophy (in Fragment 47 according to the numbering by Seibt and Vincent, see Bibliography): 'It is impossible that three hypostases can unite ... in one monad!' Here he puts his finger on a weak point of Origen's doctrine of the Trinity: Origen did not succeed, or did not convincingly succeed, in demonstrating how the three divine hypostases can be one God. That the three are one through harmony and identity of will, as Origen taught, could not content a strict monotheist. In Marcellus's view, at any rate, one cannot start from three hypostases but only from the divine unity, the monad. Of course, like other Christians Marcellus, too, knows the triad 'Father, Son and Spirit', but this triad takes its beginning from the monad. Marcellus put it like this (in Fragment 48): 'The monad spreads into a triad, but without ever suffering separation'

– a unique formulation: what is meant by the 'spreading' of the monad into a triad?

Possibly this notion is to be derived from Neopythagorean mathematics (this is Klaus Seibt's thesis). Pythagoras, a sixth-century BC philosopher, influenced later philosophical schools with his investigations into mathematics and the theory of harmony. Around the turn of the eras there was then a revival of Pythagorean philosophy which above all had an effect on the Neoplatonism dominant in the Roman Empire from the middle of the third century. The Neopythagoreans had investigated the nature of number and established references between arithmetic and geometry. Accordingly, at the level of geometry the number one corresponds to the point which is without extension, indivisible and utterly simple. If we extend the point, that produces the line, which corresponds to two; this number is no longer simple, but composite, i.e. extended and divisible. Geometrically the number three comes into being not by extending the line still further, but by broadening the line arising from the point. In geometry that produces the figure of the triangle, and a surface comes into being which becomes visible; this was not yet the case with the line, since the line has no breadth and in principle is invisible. However, the triangle still has its origin and apex in the point. It is potentially already contained in the point, but is realized only through the extension and can also again be reduced to the point from which it emerged. Marcellus must have thought of the extension of the divine monad into the triad in a similar way.

According to the Bishop of Ancyra, the divine monad can *appear* as a triad through the activity of God in creation and salvation history. Only through visible external activity does the distinction of the Son and Spirit from the Father become evident, yet they remain united in the divine monad (like the triangle in the point). There is no division, no separation of the one in the three, nor is there any juxtaposition of three independent entities: the monad spreads only to the triad, and the one appears as three.

This theory remotely recalls the modalism of the Monarchians, according to which Father and Son are only manifestations of the one God. Marcellus's opponents immediately drew this parallel and vilified Marcellus's christ-ology with the name of a famous or notorious modalist from the end of the second century and beginning of the third, namely Sabellius. To be a Sabellian was the worst charge that one could level against the Bishop of Ancyra. However, this charge was not wholly justified, since for Marcellus the divine monad is in itself a *differentiated* unity; it is Father, Logos and Spirit at the same time.

The Logos, which is God's very own inner Logos, appears outwardly in creation and thus can be 'distinguished' from the Father. According to Marcellus one can call his emergence from the monad to create the world the 'begetting before the ages' (cf. Fragment 66). Thus in this context 'begetting' does not mean ontological 'causation' or even the 'origin' of the Logos through the Father, for the Logos is eternally one with God. Rather, *'begetting'* means the *sending* of the Logos to be *active externally*. Only in this activity is the Logos to some degree 'outside' the Father; he is perceptible as Logos without the monad being divided and separated. For despite his activity in creation and later in the incarnation, at the same time the Logos remains as a power in the Father. The same is true of the Spirit (cf. Fragments 48f.): in his sending, the Spirit appears externally as Holy Spirit (not as Father, not as Son) through his activity. Nevertheless the divine monad is not divided by this, because God remains unchanged Father, Logos and Spirit.

Beyond doubt Marcellus's scheme (which he sought to support with the bold exegesis of disputed passages of scripture such as Col. 1.15 and Prov. 8.22–25) was marked by special originality and creativity. The response which such theological creativity provoked is another matter. Marcellus predominantly reaped criticism, not only for his unusual conception of monotheism but also because of his conviction that the kingdom of Christ, the incarnate Son of God, would one day have an end (cf. Fragments 102–109). Strictly speaking, this doctrine simply represented the consistent continuation of his theology: if the divine monad appears as triad only in order to create, redeem and consummate the world, this 'spreading into a triad' will come to an end when the work is done. Then the incarnate Logos, who hitherto could be distinguished from the Father by his activity in the flesh, will also return and again be in God as he was before the creation of the world.

Marcellus teaches that the incarnation did not take place so that the *Logos* could benefit from it; it took place *for our sake*, for the sake of human beings and the world. Therefore the saving plan of the incarnation has a limit: it ends when its goal is attained. Then the Logos will no longer be united with the flesh that he has assumed. But what then happens to the flesh, the human side of Jesus, which the Logos has assumed at the incarnation? Here Marcellus concedes his ignorance, because nothing precise can be found about this in the divine scriptures. But it is clear that then the flesh, the human side of Jesus, will no longer be necessary, because the universal rule of God will have been realized. And evidently Marcellus also feels it unthinkable that the human flesh together with the Logos should go into the divine monad, since in Marcellus's view the monad would then no longer be a real monad.

For most Christians in the East such teaching was so offensive that it even 'damaged' the Nicene Creed (which Marcellus claimed for himself) – for one could read the consequences of this creed in Marcellus's theology. For decades Marcellus remained the great obstacle to a unanimous solution to the problem of the Trinity.

Nevertheless, for some time Marcellus did not have to feel isolated. Like Athanasius, he succeeded in finding support in the West – albeit at the price of the first great schism between East and West.

CHAPTER 8

The Theological Split in the Empire

Along with some other bishops, Athanasius and Marcellus were banished to the west of the empire so that peace could finally come to the east, but Constantine died there in 337. The empire was divided between his three sons Constantine II (who died in 340), Constans and Constantius II. The relationship between the brothers was one more of rivalry than of harmony. Thus a high-handed act by the oldest of them, Constantine, who resided in Trier, allowed the banished bishops to return home (referring to the pretended will of the dead emperor); his brother Constantius, who was ruler in the East, allowed this only reluctantly, as he had to fear for peace in his part of the empire.

After unrest had indeed broken out in Alexandria and Ancyra, in 339 Athanasius and Marcellus were again driven from their episcopal sees. On their flight they arrived, independently of each other, in Rome, where they sought support from Pope Julius. The Bishop of Rome had no difficulty in assuming communion with Athanasius, but Marcellus, who had been condemned for his theology, had to demonstrate his orthodoxy by a written confession (which has been preserved in his *Letter to Julius*).

The Bishop of Ancyra acted shrewdly. First of all he accused his opponents of failing to recognize the Lord

71

Jesus Christ as God's *own* and *true* Logos and regarding him as another Logos who had come into being through God: therefore for them he was also *another* hypostasis, separate from the Father. They said that the Father existed before the Son and that there was a time when there was no Son (the old Arian thesis!); he was only a creature or a being made by God. Marcellus was able to win the Roman community over with such charges, which implicitly branded his opponents Arians. There had in fact been a Monarchian tendency to emphasize the unity of God in Roman theology for more than a century. But secondly, the linguistic problem came into play here: the Latin equivalent of the Greek term *hypostasis* was *substantia*. The two words correspond to some degree etymologically (*hypo-stasis* – *sub-stantia*), so intrinsically the translation is not wrong. But the content changes with the translation into Latin: if Eastern theology spoke of two hypostases, in Latin that amounted to a difference in substance between Father and Son. Accordingly, around 210 the first Latin trinitarian theologian, Tertullian of Carthage, had coined the slogan *una substantia*. So Marcellus did not find it difficult to mobilize the Roman community against his adversaries.

The Bishop of Ancyra was also cautious in describing his own faith. He refrained from repeating the most difficult theses of his own doctrine. Instead, at the centre of his description he put a short confession which did not touch at all on the problematic questions of the pre-existence of Christ – that could cause no trouble. Only in a precise analysis does one note Marcellus's emphases: thus the creed does not begin with the formula 'I believe in God the Father, the Almighty' but rather simply with 'I believe in God, the Almighty'. That is not of course fortuitous. For in Marcellus's theology the Almighty is not to be identified with God the *Father* but with the one God, who in himself is already Father, Logos and Spirit. But that could easily be overlooked.

The creed was framed with explanatory remarks by Marcellus: he confirmed that God's 'only begotten Son-Logos always exists with the Father, that he never had a beginning to his existence, that he really is from God, not created or made, but is for ever and reigns for ever with God the Father; his kingdom will … (according to Luke 1.33) have no end.' Here Marcellus takes a somewhat refined course, but without being deceitful. He apparently denies his offensive teaching that the kingdom of Christ will have an end. But in truth here he is not speaking of the eternal rule of Christ the incarnate. He is speaking of the eternal rule of the *Logos*, who reigns together with the Father – *this* rule will have no end. The eternal Logos is eternally in God; that he therefore also 'co-reigns' eternally is taken for granted in Marcellus's system. By contrast, the limited kingdom of the incarnate one is not mentioned at all. Instead, Marcellus moves further in the field of pre-existence christology and confirms (against the Arian thesis) that the Son really 'is God's own and true Logos … the indivisible power of God'.

Finally, in connection with the creed mentioned above, Marcellus emphasizes that the divinity of the Father and of the Son is indivisible. For anyone who wants to separate the Son or Logos from the almighty God must either believe that there are two Gods or confess that the Logos is not God. Thus Marcellus thinks that he has demonstrated the absurdity of his opponents' christology. He confirms his own position by statements from the Gospel of John: 'The Father is in me and I am in the Father' (John 10.38), 'I and the Father are one' (John 10.30), and 'Whoever has seen me has seen the Father' (John 14.9), verses which the Monarchians used as key passages a century before Marcellus.

Evidently the Roman community allowed itself to be convinced (also through statements of the legates who had represented Bishop Sylvester at the Council of Nicaea) that Marcellus was defending orthodox Nicene theology. However, Bishop Julius had not succeeded in persuading the Eastern bishops to take part in a joint synod which would take up the cases of Marcellus and Athanasius again. Certainly Julius asserted a privilege of the Bishop of Rome to have doubtful depositions looked at again, but the other side disputed this privilege and insisted on the validity of the verdicts of deposition against Athanasius and Marcellus, which had been given legitimately at the synods of Tyre in

335 and Constantinople in 336. So at the beginning of 341 a synod took place in Rome without Eastern participation; its verdict rehabilitated Marcellus and Athanasius and at the same time accused the theologians of the East of being 'Arians'.

The East was put under pressure by the intervention of Rome. The Eastern bishops, who assembled in Antioch in 341 for the dedication of a church, used this synod (known under the name 'Dedication' or 'Encaenia' Synod) to reformulate their faith and thus also go beyond the Nicene Creed theologically. That would not have been opportune during the lifetime of Constantine I, but Constantine had been dead for four years. However, not just one new creed but four different formulae are associated with the Synod of Antioch.

Whereas the so-called third Antiochene formula (handed down in Athanasius, *On the Synods* 24.2–5) has to be regarded as the private confession of a bishop who had to demonstrate his orthodoxy before the synod, the so-called first Antiochene formula (a relative short scheme) reacts to the charges of the West (see Athanasius, *On the Synods* 22.3–7): the Eastern bishops state right at the beginning that they are in no way followers of Arius. How could they as bishops follow someone who is only a presbyter? In content the formula is insignificant, because it does not adopt any clear position over disputed questions.

The extensive second Antiochene formula (quoted in Athanasius, *On the Synods* 23.2–10) is more important: after the confession of the 'one God Father, the Almighty', here again the statements on christological pre-existence are decisive: the bishops name the one Lord Jesus Christ:

> ... the only-begotten God (John 1.18) ... who was begotten before the ages from the Father, God from God, whole from whole, sole from sole, perfect from perfect, King from King and Lord from Lord; (he is) Living Logos, Living Wisdom, true Light, Way, Truth, Resurrection, Shepherd, Door, unchangeable and unalterable; unchanged image of the substance (Greek *ousia*) of the Godhead, of the Counsel, the Power and Glory of the Father; the firstborn of all creation (Col. 1.15), who was in the beginning with

God (in Greek with the article), God Logos (without the article) ... by whom all things were made (cf. John 1.1–3), and in whom all things consist ...

The statements are recognizably concerned to provide biblical legitimation. They cite a series of New Testament titles for Christ, the majority of which come from the Fourth Gospel. With John 1.18 and Col. 1.15 the position of the Logos as mediator between the Father and creation is worked out dialectically – as happened in the creed of Eusebius of Caesarea at the Council of Nicaea. The reference to John 1.1–3 is meant to emphasize the biblical differentiation between the Father as God with the article (i.e. God in the absolute sense) and the Logos as God without the article (i.e. God in the derived sense) – a distinction to which Origen had already drawn attention in his *Commentary on John* (and Justin before him), in order to attest the subordination of the Logos to the absolute God.

The redundant list of statements about origin ('God from God, etc.') is striking; it is meant to express as clearly as possible that both the Father and the pre-existent Son are each intrinsically whole and perfect: they do not coincide in any way, nor do they belong together as parts of a greater whole. The Father is one, and the Son begotten by him is likewise one. Thus the distinct entities of the Father and the Son are described as two hypostases.

That is underlined once again when after their confession of Father, Son and Spirit the bishops quote the command of the risen Christ to baptize in Matt. 28.19 and explain that baptism takes place in the name of

> ... the Father who is truly Father, the Son who is truly Son, and the Holy Spirit who is truly Holy Spirit, the names (Father, Son, Spirit) not being given without meaning or effect, but denoting accurately the peculiar hypostasis, rank (Greek *taxis*), and glory of those who are named, so that they are three in hypostasis, and in harmony (Greek *symphonia*) one.

This figure of biblical argumentation likewise occurs in the creed of Eusebius of Caesarea at the Council of Nicaea and again in Arius's 'reconciliation creed'. But this time it is used explicitly as a foundation for the doctrine of three hypostases, and in a subordinationist sense: accordingly the sequence 'Father, Son, Spirit' in Matt. 28.18 is not random, but means that the hypostasis of the Father has a higher rank and greater glory than that of the Son, while the hypostasis of the Holy Spirit is even lower in rank and glory than the Son. However, so as not to leave the unity of the three hypostases unmentioned (and thus be open to attack), reference is made to their harmony. Thus basically this is merely a repetition of the position of Origen, which he had already worked out a century earlier. It is evident from this pale formulation that even in 341 Eastern theology had not yet overcome its traditional 'defect' (in conceptualizing the unity of Father, Son and Spirit).

By contrast, the attempt to define the relationship between the two hypostases Father and Son more closely by the category of 'image' in the sense that Christ is characterized as the 'unchanged image' of the Father is worth noting. It means that Father and Son correspond in every respect, but are distinct in their own existences: they are two and not one. And despite the total correspondence between image and original there is again a subordinationist element in this description. For according to the dominant philosophy of the time an image, as a copy, is by nature less than its model, the original.

In order to protect their confession from misinterpretation, the bishops in Antioch finally dissociated themselves from 'any heretical false teaching': they pronounced an anathema on anyone who taught that there was a time, or moment, or age before the Son was begotten. They likewise anathematized the doctrine that the Son is

> a creature as one of the (other) creatures, or an offspring as one of the (other) offsprings, or something made as one of the (other) things that are made (which not even Arius had asserted).

With this text the position of the East on trinitarian theology was fixed for a long time. It is to be described as a three-hypostases doctrine and as (moderate) subordinationism (following Origen and Eusebius of Caesarea): the label 'Arian' is misleading, as the Eastern theologians did not repeat the radical theses of Arius and to all appearances did not share them. By contrast, the second Antiochene formula had nothing to do with the Nicene Creed; rather, it was to be a substitute for this creed which had been discredited by the teaching of Marcellus.

Finally, the so-called fourth Antiochene formula in reality came into being only some months after the Dedication Synod: it was thought of as the basis for the theological union of East and West and was entrusted to a small delegation of bishops who were to go directly to Constans, the emperor of the West. However, they did not meet him in the imperial residence of Trier. The creed (which can be read in Athanasius, *On the Synods* 25.2–5) was conceived of as a compromise, since it passed over both the doctrine of three hypostases and the Eastern image theology so as not to give new occasion for dispute. The affirmative statements are cautiously formulated; only at one point does the text become clear: the kingdom of the risen and exalted Christ is described as 'infinite', 'it lasts for endless ages, for he shall be seated on the right hand of the Father, not only in this age but in that, too, which is to come'. This is an implicit attack on Marcellus of Ancyra, but in order to provide balance at the end the text condemns Arianism in the form of the assertion that the Son is out of nothing or from another hypostasis and not from God and that there was once a time when he was not. Thus the tendency of the compromise text is clear: the proposal of the East sought to rule out extreme positions – on the one hand the doctrine of Arius and on the other that of Marcellus of Ancyra. Moreover the Eastern bishops wanted to show themselves conciliatory. However, their proposal proved totally ineffective.

The situation seemed confused: East and West were not only divided in church politics but also split theologically and incapable of union on their own. For this reason the bishops around Julius of Rome and Athanasius sought political support from Emperor Constans, the ruler of the western half of the empire, in order to get things moving again.

CHAPTER 9

Serdica – the Failed Imperial Council

The plan which the Emperor Constans put to his brother Constantius, the ruler of the East, was orientated on that of their dead father Constantine: as in 325, the unity of the church was to be brought about through an ecumenical council. Constantius, who because of constant wars with the Persians, the 'arch-enemies' of the empire, was time and again dependent on military support from his brother, agreed with this project. The city of Serdica (present-day Sofia in Bulgaria) was decided on as the place of the conference.

The council met, probably in autumn 342. As planned, numerous bishops from East and West took part, among the latter being Bishop Ossius of Cordoba, who had already taken part in the Council of Nicaea. The banished bishops Athanasius and Marcellus travelled with the representatives of the West. However, Pope Julius of Rome did not appear – he followed the example of his predecessor and sent only legates to Serdica.

Given the presuppositions, this gathering of bishops could have been an ecumenical council, as intended, but the plan failed from the start: the bishops of the East refused to take part in joint sessions as long as Marcellus of Ancyra and Athanasius of Alexandria were present. In

the Eastern view, both had been legitimately condemned
and deposed and therefore had no right to take part in
discussion of affairs of the church at a council. However,
the Western bishops referred to the rehabilitation of their
two colleagues by the Roman synod of 341. Initiatives once
again to clarify the accusations against Athanasius failed.
And when the news arrived that Emperor Constantius had
won a victory over the Persians in the East and his hands
were no longer tied, the bishops of the region which he
ruled ventured to leave the council. Before they did, they
composed a text to justify their action (the Latin translation
has been handed down in Hilary, *Collectanea antiariana
Parisina* A IV); in the disputed questions of faith they also
referred to the fourth Antiochene formula, which a year
previously should already have served as a basis for union.
In addition, the Eastern bishops once again condemned
extreme theological positions, such as the doctrine 'that
there are three Gods or that Christ is not God; that neither
Christ nor the Son of God existed before the ages, or that
one and the same is Father, Son and Holy Spirit; that the
Son is unbegotten or that the Father did not beget the
Son by decision and will'. These anathemas were to be
a defence against the suspicion of tritheism, and on the
other side a rejection of Marcellus's peculiar conception of
monotheism, according to which the begetting of the Son
was not to be understood as internal to the Trinity but was
to refer only to his external activity. In this way the bishops
of the East believed that they had sufficiently safeguarded
their theological position, and they left.

The assembly of Western bishops continued to meet in
Serdica. It had set itself two tasks: first, to safeguard the
rehabilitation of Athanasius and other deposed bishops
legally (this was stated in the famous Canon 3 of Serdica,
through which the Bishop of Rome was recognized as
an authority of appeal in church disputes); secondly, the
bishops of the West, too, now wanted to give binding
expression to their faith and to publish it in an encyclical
(text and German translation in Ulrich, *Anfänge*, pp. 51–59,
see Bibliography).

The document first attacks those who recognize Christ as God but not as *true* God and do not even regard him as *true* Son, because they interpret his begetting as 'coming into being' and attribute to him a beginning before all time – this is a condemnation not only of the original teaching of Arius but also of the position of the majority of Eastern theologians, who had again given up the key Nicene clarifications of the *true divinity* of the Son, his being begotten *from the substance of the Father*, and his being *consubstantial with the Father*.

The 'heretical' view that the hypostases of the Father, the Son and the Holy Spirit are different and separate is also criticized; against this the bishops teach:

> There is (only) one hypostasis of the Father, the Son and the Holy Spirit, which the heretics for their part also call *ousia* (substance). And if they ask who or what the hypostasis of the Son is, it is manifestly the same as that of the only Father. At the same time we say that the Father never was without the Son nor the Son without the Father … It is utter nonsense to say that once the Father was not Father … Indeed the witness of the Son himself is that 'I am in the Father and the Father is in me' (John 14.10) and 'I and the Father are one' (John 10.30).

Here a one-hypostasis doctrine is set against the three-hypostases doctrine of the East, which first betrays the hand of Marcellus and secondly also sums up the traditional Monarchian tendency of the West. Again it should be noted that the Greek term *hypostasis* could be rendered in Latin with *substantia* and that the Latin West was accustomed to speak of the one divine substance; this was regarded as synonymous with the Greek talk of one divine hypostasis as put forward, say, by Marcellus of Ancyra (similarly with recourse to John 14.10 and John 10.30). It also becomes clear that here the terms *hypostasis* and *ousia* are regarded as synonyms and are referred in the singular to God.

The members of the synod also make it clear that no one denies the begetting (of the Son); however, it does not mean 'begetting as a creature' (as Arius had interpreted it) but begetting 'as the shaper of archangels and angels, the world and the human race' – Marcellus's teaching of the 'begetting' of the Logos to external creative activity seems to appear between the lines here. It is also said that this begetting can have nothing to do with a 'beginning of being', 'because the God Logos who always is knows no beginning and no end'.

The Western bishops went on to seek to guard themselves against the charge of modalistic Sabellianism:

> We do not say that the Father is Son nor that the Son is Father. But the Father is Father and the Son is Son of the Father. We confess that the Son is the power (Greek *dynamis*) of the Father. We confess the Logos of God the Father, alongside whom there is no other, and this Logos as true God, wisdom and power. We teach him as true Son ...

The statement that the Father and the Son are not identical does not sound very convincing as a mere assertion, since the existence of each as a distinct hypostasis had been denied; the next statement further accentuates the problem. That the Son was said to be the *dynamis* of the Father, the potency of God (for creating and redeeming the world), must have seemed to confirm the worst fears of the Eastern bishops. Is the Son 'only' a potency of the Father? Does he possess no being of his own? In statements with which one side thought that it was defending monotheism, the others immediately suspected the danger of modalism – this was the dilemma of the controversy.

In order to invalidate the *biblical* arguments of the opposing side, the bishops of the West also had to take up the christological titles in John 1.18 and Col. 1.15 which in the conception of the Eusebians dialectically expressed the ontological mediating position of the pre-existent Logos: from the side of God he was the 'only-begotten', from the side of the creatures, however, he was the 'firstborn of all creation'. The members of the synod in Serdica differed:

> We confess the only-begotten (John 1.18) and the firstborn (Col. 1.15) – as only-begotten but the Logos, who always was and is in the Father. However, (the title) firstborn

refers to the man (i.e. Jesus) and the new creation, as (Jesus) too is firstborn from the dead (Col. 1.18).

Thus the two titles are assigned to different levels of christology. Since in the Western view the eternal Logos in God (the 'only-begotten') cannot be 'firstborn of all creation', *this* title must be interpreted in a different way, i.e. soteriologically: it is not the Logos in himself but the *incarnate one* who is the firstborn of the (new) creation – this is the bold exegesis which goes back to Marcellus of Ancyra.

Jesus's saying in John 14.28, 'the Father is greater than I', caused another exegetical problem: the Eastern theologians were fond of quoting it to justify their subordinationist christology. The bishops of the West also had to react to this:

> None (of us) ever denies the statement: 'The Father is greater than I' – but that does not apply to another hypostasis or any difference but (only) because the name of the Father is in itself greater than that of the Son.

However, this explanation in truth shows up a serious defect in the theology of Marcellus and the West which is influenced by him. Here the distinction between Father, Son and Spirit in God seems possible only through the differentiation of the 'names'; evidently they do not have another category at their disposal.

In their counter-move, the bishops of the West attack the inadequate notion that the Eusebians (following Origen) had of the divine unity, namely that Father and Son are one (cf. John 10.30) on the basis of their harmony and equal disposition. From the perspective of the West that meant that in theory there could also be disunity or a difference of opinion between Father and Son as among human beings. To this manifest nonsense the bishops of the West opposed their own view that the unity of the Father and the Son is grounded in the unity of the hypostasis, which is the one hypostasis of the Father and the Son.

In connection with that, the bishops in Serdica confirm that the Son rules together with the Father without beginning or end, for what is everlasting has never begun its being nor can it end. The assertion of the eternal kingdom of the Son apparently rectifies the christology of Marcellus of Ancyra; however, appearances are deceptive – even Marcellus could subscribe to this statement because here he was thinking of the eternal co-regency of the *Logos in God*, not of the kingdom of the *incarnate* Christ. And probably the statement of the Western bishops also meant this, since they denied that the kingdom of the Son had a beginning – and at least that cannot be true of the incarnate one.

The text of Serdica ends with statements about the Holy Spirit, the incarnation and the difference between the unity of believers in God and the (ontological) unity of Father and Logos.

All in all, one cannot disguise the overwhelming influence of Marcellus of Ancyra on the creed of Serdica. Marcellus was probably the most outstanding theologian of this group, even before Athanasius, and far more the bishops of the West; moreover he had taken part in the Council of Nicaea, in whose orthodox (anti-Arian) tradition the assembly of bishops in Serdica saw itself. Who then could have better explained the intentions and consequences of Nicene doctrine than Marcellus? However, in truth the creed of Serdica represented a new interpretation and supposed improvement of the Nicene Creed, because it answered questions which had been left open and tied the Western church to the doctrine of the one divine hypostasis. As the resolutions of Serdica were disseminated in the Western provinces of the empire and were signed by many bishops, we may assume that most churches of the West first got to know the Nicene faith through its interpretation in the creed of Serdica, and for a long time identified it with the one-hypostasis doctrine. In the history of dogma this doctrine is described as the 'old Nicene position', to indicate that it was later developed and changed.

The real explosiveness of this evaluation lies in the recognition that at this time – in 342 – *none* of the disputing parties had already reached the theological stage which some decades later was to become the binding tradition of the church. The old cliché that the history of dogma is exhausted in defending the truth handed down against new heresies does not apply here. Elements of the truth are to be found on *both* sides, and the concern of *both* sides is understandable: on the one hand a consistent insistence on the divine unity and the true divinity of the saviour, and on the other an emphasis on the distinct reality and specific existence of the Father and the Son and the Holy Spirit, which may not be curtailed in a nominalistic way. The solution to the problem was not yet in view: first it had to be found and fought for. In Serdica there was a failure here.

However, the problems which had not really been discussed thoroughly at the Council of Nicaea were now openly on the table. How are unity and trinity in God to be regarded? Is there only one divine hypostasis, as the West taught, or are there three, as the East taught? In the first instance, what is the distinction between Father, Son and Spirit? The problem of the West lay in demonstrating that. Conversely, how can the unity of three hypostases be demonstrated? The East did not come up with a convincing answer. Here the problem was not only identified, but awareness of it was sharpened on both sides.

But for the moment the fronts had hardened. For a while Emperor Constantius even cordoned off his half of the empire from the West. Nevertheless, the efforts to resolve the conflict did not end with the failed Council of Serdica. In subsequent years delegations of bishops went to and fro to sound out the situation in the different parts of the empire. There were small movements on the fronts: because the bishops of the East saw that the West had problems with talk of three hypostases, they attempted to put the same doctrine in different terms and described Father, Son and Spirit as three persons (*prosopa*) or in a makeshift way as three 'things' (*pragmata*, in the sense of entities) – thus in the so-called *Ekthesis makrostichos*, the 'long-lined creed' of 344 (handed down in Athanasius, *On the Synods* 26). In this way they wanted to avoid giving the impression that they were speaking of three different gods. Conversely, the bishops of the West had realized that they had come to be suspected of Sabellianism. In order to remove this suspicion, in Milan in 345 and 347 they were ready to condemn a disciple and former deacon of Marcellus by the name of Photinus, who had been made bishop of the city of Sirmium (on the Sava) and had put forward even more radical theses than his teacher. In a sense this Photinus was a pawn to be sacrificed, to relieve the Western position without at the same time compromising it. However, none of these gestures helped. The law of action therefore again shifted from the theological to the political level.

Under pressure from Constans, the emperor of the West, who even threatened war, in 346 Constantius, the ruler in the east of the empire, had to be prepared to invite Athanasius (and the other banished bishops) to return to their episcopal sees. On the journey, in 346 Athanasius met Constantius in Antioch in Syria and sought to gain complete rehabilitation from him. However, the emperor did not want to humiliate himself so deeply – he saw the recall of the deposed bishop as an act of grace (which of course could be revoked). Within a short time Athanasius had again gained control in Egypt and had even found new allies (for example in Palestine). But Constantius did not forgive Athanasius for stirring up Emperor Constans against him and the return to Alexandria.

CHAPTER 10

Constantius II and the Quest for a Theological Compromise

The opportunity to get new scope for action against Athanasius arose when in 350 Emperor Constans fell victim to the usurper Magnentius, who had him murdered when fleeing. Granted, it took another three years for Constantius to defeat the rebel and secure sole rule in the empire, but from 353 he could devote himself unhindered to implementing his goals in religious politics without having to take account of a rival. Constantius II – in continuity with his father Constantine – saw himself called by God as Roman emperor to restore and safeguard the unity of religion. Disruption of the peace could not be tolerated.

As early as 351 a synod in Sirmium in the presence of the emperor deposed Marcellus's disciple Photinus, who hitherto had tenaciously defended his see; the synod also published a creed (handed down e.g. in Athanasius, *On the Synods* 27) which was in the tradition of the fourth Antiochene formula and the declaration of the Eastern bishops in Serdica, but had been expanded by a series of doctrinal condemnations (anathemas). Some of these were directed against Arian theses (e.g. the origin of the Son out of nothing or the fact that he once did not exist), but above all they were against the theology of Marcellus and Photinus. Thus, for example, the statement was condemned 'that the substance (Greek *ousia*) of the Godhead spreads or retracts', and likewise the thesis 'that Father, Son and Holy Spirit are one person (*prosopon*)'.

Athanasius, who on top of everything else was suspected of having conspired with the usurper Magnentius, also remained in the emperor's sights: at two synods in Arles in 353 and Milan in 355 Constantius compelled another condemnation of the Bishop of Alexandria by Western bishops (among whom Athanasius had most support). Anyone who opposed this move was banished to the East. As well as Dionysius of Milan and Lucifer of Calaris (on Sardinia), Pope Liberius of Rome was also exiled; he had not taken part in the synods, but was summoned to the imperial court in Milan and put under pressure there. Because the pope refused to drop Athanasius, in 356 he too was banished, to Thrace. The same year the emperor decided to use force against Athanasius to drive him from his episcopal see. However, the Bishop of Alexandria was able to avoid arrest and hid himself among the monks in the Egyptian desert. In 356 Bishop Hilary of Poitiers became another victim of church politics; he was condemned at a synod in Biterrae (Béziers) in Gaul on allegedly political grounds. However, he used his exile in the East to develop his own view of Eastern theology and to communicate to the West the insights that he had gained.

From the time that Constantius II defined the religious policy of the empire, the majority party of the Eastern bishops seemed to keep the upper hand in the struggle over the theology of the Trinity. But it now proved that the joint resistance against the Nicenes and the theology of the West coloured by Marcellus had been the strongest bond that held the East together. For precisely now, when no further threat was to be expected from outside, the majority party split into different groups which interpreted the doctrine of the three hypostases and the subordination of the Logos to the Father – hitherto the common denominator of Eastern theology – in quite different ways.

The first sign of this was the revival of Arianism, which was thought to be dead, in the 350s. This new version of

Arianism, which is also called Neo-Arianism, is above all associated with two names, those of the Syrian Aetius and his disciple Eunomius, who was to become bishop of the city of Cyzicus in Asia Minor.

Aetius had been ordained deacon in Antioch in 350/351. From Arius he took over the view that only the unbegotten God could be true God. Aetius associated this conviction with a particular kind of linguistic philosophy according to which the substance of things can be described exactly and rendered by human designations. According to Aetius the substance (the *ousia*) of the true God could also be conceptualized precisely, with the term unbegottenness (Greek *agennesia*). That and that alone comprised the substance of the true God. By contrast, according to church teaching the Logos/Son is begotten, so his substance does not consist in unbegottenness but in begottenness. Now if the substance of the true God can be defined as unbegottenness and the substance of the Logos as begottenness, it follows that the substance of the one and the substance of the other cannot be the same, since unbegottenness is diametrically opposed to begottenness. That proves with scientific exactitude that the Father and the Son are not *homoousios*, of the same substance, but decidedly *heteroousios*, i.e. different in substance. To put it another way: the substance of the Son is not the same as the substance of the Father; it is dissimilar (Greek *anhomoios*, which gave this party the designation 'Anhomoeans'). A further anti-Nicene consequence of their doctrine was that the Son could not be begotten *from the substance of the Father*, since unbegottenness could not of course be handed on. Instead of this, the Son derives from the *activity* of the Father, he is made by him – and with this we are back to Arius's old thesis that the Son is a creature: a special creature, but nevertheless created or made by God.

The new version, and even more the 'scholarly' underpinning and radicalization of Arian theology, could not meet with undivided approval among the bishops of the East. Most had honestly distanced themselves from the radical theses of Arius; they did not feel that they were Arians and had time and again asserted as much to the

West. If Aetius and his followers now put forward the 'proof' that the Son was only 'something made' and ontologically of *quite a different* substance from the Father, they inevitably felt compromised.

In reaction there was a theological counter-movement in the East, whose spokesmen were Bishop Basil of Ancyra (since 336 the successor to the deposed Marcellus) and George of Laodicea. This group maintained the Eastern doctrine of the three divine hypostases, but at the same time wanted to demarcate itself clearly from Arianism. Whereas the Neo-Arians now used the concept of begetting to express the difference in substance between the unbegotten Father and the begotten Son, Basil of Ancyra and George of Laodicea referred to this biblically legitimized metaphor (cf. Ps. 2.7; Heb. 1.4; 5.5; Ps. 110.3 or 109.3 LXX), with the opposite intention: since the metaphor of 'begetting' comes from the world of experience, its hidden sense is also to be sought there. Now in the world of experience a father (human or animal) always has offspring who are like him in substance. Precisely the same is also meant when in the case of God one speaks of 'begetting' in the metaphorical sense – for as a matter of course here one must guard against any idea of sexuality and passion. If God is called the 'Father' of the Logos/'Son' (these, too, are basically metaphors from the world of experience), that can only mean that he has brought forth the Son as a being who corresponds to and is like his own being.

The bishops around Basil of Ancyra and George of Laodicea taught precisely this: while by comparison with the Father the Son is a distinct hypostasis and has his own being (*ousia*) as individual substance, precisely because he is 'begotten' by the Father (in a metaphorical sense), his *ousia* corresponds to the *ousia* of the Father. Thus the term 'begetting' does not focus, as with the neo-Arians, on the radical otherness of the Father and the Son, but specifically on their correspondence in substance.

This answer to Neo-Arianism can be summed up in the statement 'The Son is like or similar to the Father in substance (Greek *homoios kat'ousian*).' One can also express the relation of the Son to the Father with the adjective *homoiousios*, so in the history of dogma the representatives of this doctrine are designated Homoeousians. It is striking how close the term *homoiousios* (of like or similar substance) comes to the Nicene *homoousios* (of the same substance or one in substance); sometimes scholars ironically commented that the two adjectives differed by only one letter. For tactical reasons, the bishops around Basil of Ancyra and George of Laodicea had wanted to tone down the hard Nicene *homoousios* and therefore did not confess the *identity* of substance but only the *similarity* of substance of the Son with the Father. However, this interpretation failed to take the point of the Homoeousian solution to the problem.

The two Greek adjectives *homos* and *homoios* largely have the same meaning: they express likeness but with different nuances. *homos* can mean 'like' in the sense of identical, *homoios* 'like' in the sense of similar, because two things which are 'like' each other are not therefore identical with each other. And precisely that was the issue: according to traditional Eastern teaching God the Father and God the Son cannot be identical with each other, since that would be modalistic thinking. Rather, they are two distinct hypostases, but each has his own *ousia*, individual substance. Nevertheless, because of his 'begetting', the substance of the Son is like the substance of the Father – so he is *homoiousios*. With this definition the Homoeousians attempted to combine the distinct reality of the hypostases of Father and Son with the likeness of their respective substance.

Emperor Constantius was also anxious about the rise of Neo-Arianism. It was clear to him that personal political measures alone could not safeguard peace in the church; a theological solution to the disputed questions also had to be found. During the expansion of his rule westwards Constantius had increasingly come under the influence of Illyrian bishops (Valens of Mursa, Ursacius of Singidinum and Germinius of Sirmium) who gave themselves a privileged place as 'court bishops' surrounding the emperor and functioned as his advisers. With their support, in 357 Constantius organized a small synod in Sirmium which was to give the discussion a new direction, in order to make it possible to bring the different standpoints closer together.

The new line of this so-called second formula of Sirmium (handed down e.g. in Hilary, *On the Synods* 11) ended up in bracketing off the greatest problem from the start:

> The question of the substance (of Father and Son), which in Greek is called *ousia*, has disturbed some, namely the discussion over the *homoousios* or the *homoiousios*. Therefore this matter shall no longer be mentioned and no one shall preach on it, because it is not discussed in the holy scriptures, because it goes beyond human knowledge and no one can explain the generation of the Son ... Manifestly only the Father knows how he has begotten his Son, and the Son how he was begotten from the Father.

This ban on speaking expresses the insight that no agreement can be aimed at in the debate over the substance of Father and Son – consequently it seems better to break off the discussion, although this has to be disguised theologically.

At the same time the second formula of Sirmium puts forward a firm position on the theology of the Trinity, according to which there is only one God and his only Son Jesus Christ; there are not two Gods – after all, Jesus himself calls the Father 'my God' in John 20.17. It is further taught (with John 14.28) that the Father is greater than the Son (in honour, dignity, glory, majesty and also through the name 'Father') and the Son is subject to the Father, moreover that of these 'two persons' the Father has no beginning but the Son is born of the Father. And finally, the command to baptize in Matt. 28.19 confirms that one must always hold firm to the Trinity.

In these statements Eastern subordinationism is formulated relatively abruptly. The existence of three hypostases is also defended indirectly, though the term itself is avoided. Even the Arian position glimmers between the lines, namely that only the Father with no beginning can be the one (true) God, because the Son is born/begotten. All in all, however, the formula seeks to circumnavigate the most difficult terminological rocks (the 'substance' of God and the 'three hypostases', the Logos as 'image' of the Father or even as 'perfect creature' are not mentioned) yet nevertheless express the theological tradition of the East. This proposed solution was given weight first by the authority of the emperor and in addition by the fact that it succeeded in moving the *eminence grise* of the Western episcopate, Bishop Ossius of Cordoba, who was almost a hundred years old, to sign, along with Pope Liberius, who had been worn down by his two years of exile in Thrace. The pope had already dropped Athanasius, without in recompense being allowed to return to Rome; now he also signed the new formula of faith – a tremendous gain in prestige for the emperor's cause and a lasting loss of face for the pope, who was vigorously criticized by the loyal adherents to the Nicene Creed.

The initiative of the emperor and his court bishops also met with resistance, for example among some Western bishops, but above all from the group of Homoeousians, in whose view the formula of Sirmium did not counter the danger of Neo-Arianism resolutely enough but rather promoted it. Therefore this group propagated its own theology as the better concept: church faith confesses 'Father' and 'Son' and uses the metaphor of 'begetting' to indicate that the Son is like or similar in substance (*homoiousios*) to the Father. It does so to reject both Neo-Arianism, which asserted a dissimilarity in substance between Father and Son, and at the same time also the Nicene *homoousios*, which ended up in the identity of substance (Greek *tautoousios*) of Father and Son.

In the Homoeousian view even the problematical passage of scripture Prov. 8.22–25, which from the beginning had played a central role in the Arian argument, was compatible with this doctrine: the statements 'The Lord created me [viz., the Logos/Son] as the beginning of his ways' and 'before all the hills he begets me' are to be understood dialectically, each interpreting the other. Talk of begetting proves that the Son is not a creature. But conversely, the statement that he was created protects against a false (all too natural) understanding of 'begetting', as if the Father had given away something of his own substance and in this way had 'propagated' himself. Both statements had to be held in the right balance so as not to distort the truth.

Moreover the spokesman of the Homoeousians, Bishop Basil of Ancyra, himself had good relations with the emperor and hoped to win him over to his own cause. This marked the beginning of a tug-of-war for the ruler's favour. In 358 the Homoeousians gained the upper hand over the court bishops and laid down their position in the third formula of Sirmium. But only a year later the court bishops repeated their claim to leadership. In all these fluctuations Emperor Constantius did not give up his attempts to restore church unity. He had the idea of holding an ecumenical council, of the kind that his father Constantine had held in Nicaea. To prepare for this council of the whole empire, he brought the rival groups of the court bishops and the Homoeousians round the table in Sirmium. They were to work out a joint creed which was to serve as the basis for the council negotiations.

Amazingly, the rivals agreed on a joint text, the so-called fourth formula of Sirmium, dated 22 May 359 (also called the 'dated creed', handed down by Athanasius, *On the Synods* 8.4–7). Its decisive passages run:

> We believe in one only and true God the Father, Almighty, Creator and Framer of all things; And in one only-begotten Son of God, who, before all ages, and before any beginning, and before all conceivable time, and before all comprehensible being, was begotten impassibly from God: through whom the ages were disposed and all things were made; and him begotten as the only-begotten, the only from the only Father, God from God, like (or similar to) the Father who begat him according to the Scriptures; whose generation no one knows, except the Father alone who begat him ...

Statements follow about the incarnation and the Holy Spirit, and the creed ends with a declaration of principle:

> But whereas the term 'substance' (*ousia*) was adopted by the Fathers in too much simplicity, and gave offence because it was unknown to the people, and is not contained in the

Scriptures, it has seemed good [to us] to remove it, that the term 'substance' (*ousia*) be never in any case used of God again, because the divine Scriptures nowhere speak of the 'substance' (*ousia*) of Father and Son. But we say that the Son is like (or similar to) the Father in every respect, as also the Holy Scriptures say and teach.

The text clearly indicates the theological compromise between the court bishops and the Homoeousians around Basil of Ancyra and George of Laodicea: the abrupt subordinationism of the second formula of Sirmium is notably toned down; moreover the absolute pre-existence of the begotten Son before all time is emphasized. Above all it is taught that the Son is like or similar to (Greek *homoios*) the Father, but there is no mention of substance because the text (like the second formula of Sirmium) is generally against using the disputed term *ousia* any longer. How intensive the struggle for this compromise had been is evident in particular from the last formulation, which states a likeness/similarity *in every respect* between Father and Son. Precisely because the Homoeousians renounced speaking of a likeness/similarity *in substance* of the Father and the Son for the sake of peace, they attached particular importance to this generalization: if 'correspondence in every respect' was taught in respect of Father and Son, the correspondence in substance was also subsumed under this formula, and no one could any longer claim, as the Neo-Arians did, that the Son was dissimilar (*anhomoios*) to the Father in any respect.

But this very point was again a thorn in the flesh for the court bishops. They aimed to win as many theologians as possible over to this compromise text. As long as there was an indeterminate statement about some similarity or likeness of the Son to the Father, the Neo-Arians could also agree, with the inner reservation that this similarity or likeness did not extend to the substance. Thus Neo-Arians had no difficulty, for example, in assuming a similarity in will and activity between Father and Son – the 'harmony' of the two hypostases was in fact traditional doctrine in the East. By contrast, if there was to be likeness *in every respect*, it was made almost impossible for the Neo-Arians to assent to the text. So one of the court bishops attempted to express his reservations in signing the formula. He added to his signature a remark in which he confessed the similarity or likeness of the Son to the Father only quite generally, without the addition '*in every respect*'. The emperor did not let this pass. However, now Basil of Ancyra also explained his signing by emphasizing that the similarity or likeness of the Son to the Father extended to everything, and therefore did not just concern the will, but also the hypostasis and the being (Greek *einai*). Certainly Basil carefully avoided the forbidden term *ousia*; nevertheless, everyone knew what he meant. Here already the fragility of this theological compromise becomes evident: it brackets out the really controversial questions and aims only at the smallest common denominator.

However, first of all this compromise was fully established, thanks to the skill of the imperial management. Constantius and his advisers were aware that there could be an explosion if the Western and the Eastern bishops were summoned to the same council – that had already been experienced about fifteen years previously in Serdica. In order to avoid this explosion it had been resolved not to convene a joint council but to convene two separate synods for East and West. However, both part-synods would then send a delegation to the imperial court so that the results could be harmonized.

Success proved these tactics to be the right ones. The two part-synods of 359, which met in Ariminum/Rimini in Italy and in Seleucia in Isauria, would not at first accept the text of the fourth formula of Sirmium and made counter-proposals. But the delegations of the two synods were worked on by the emperor's confidential advisers until they fell in with the imperial line: the delegates from Ariminum signed a creed in Nike in Thrace which was very similar to the fourth formula of Sirmium, but in addition prohibited the Western doctrine of the one divine hypostasis. Only quite general mention was made in the text of the 'likeness' or 'similarity' between Father and Son (without the addition of '*in every respect*'). After their return to Ariminum the delegates swore the bishops waiting there to this creed, which to calm people was later flanked with some anti-Arian anathemas. With these resolutions in their pocket, a new delegation travelled to the imperial court in Constantinople, where the delegates from the synod of Seleucia (which was likewise split) were also present, and were confronted with the results of the negotiations in Ariminum and Nike.

On New Year's Eve 359/360 all the bishops present in Constantinople finally signed a creed (quoted e.g. in Athanasius, *On the Synods* 30.2–10), the decisive passages in which were little changed from the fourth formula of Sirmium and the confession of Nike:

> We believe in one God Father, Almighty, from whom are all things; and in the only-begotten Son of God, begotten from God before all ages and before any beginning, by whom all things were made, visible and invisible. He was begotten as only-begotten, the only from the only Father, God from God, like (or similar) to the Father who begat him according to the Scriptures; whose generation no one knows, except the Father alone who begat him ...

Here too the 'regulation about speaking' at the end of the text is of decisive significance:

> But concerning the term 'substance' (*ousia*), which was adopted by the Fathers in too much simplicity and, being unknown to the people, caused offence, because the Scriptures do not contain it, it has seemed good [to us] to remove it, and for the future to make no mention of it at all, since the divine Scriptures nowhere speak of the substance of Father and Son. Moreover neither ought [the term] hypostasis to be used concerning Father, Son, and Holy Spirit. But we say that the Son is like or similar to (Greek *homoios*) the Father, as the divine Scriptures say and teach.

The passing of this text was a triumph for the compromise policy of the emperor and his court bishops. By deleting the last Homoeousian accent from the creed with the general statement of the similarity or likeness between Father and Son, which was not specified further, the basis for consensus seemed broadened – even theologians who were convinced that the Son is *not in every respect* similar to the Father could sign this formula. In addition, in order finally to get out of the impasse of the theological debates, in future the hotly contested terms *ousia* and (now also) *hypostasis* should not be used at all – this regulation affected the Nicenes just as much as the Homoeousians and the Neo-Arians. To all appearances, in this way it had proved possible to bring the differing standpoints to a common denominator with the statement that the Son is (in some way) like or similar to (*homoios*) the Father. The history of dogma describes this position and the theologians who aimed at and achieved the compromise as Homoean.

A short time after it was signed, the creed was confirmed at another synod in Constantinople and put into force by imperial decree; at the same time all earlier creeds were declared to be invalid. From now on the new creed was regarded as binding on the whole imperial church (so scholars speak of the 'Homoean imperial dogma') . Bishops who did not recognize it had to give up their episcopal sees. The Homoeousian bishops had assented to the compromise formula on New Year's Eve 359/360, but now on various pretexts they were removed from their sees and replaced by more pliable theologians.

Emperor Constantius seemed to have achieved his wishes. The Homoean creed of Constantinople had laid a theological foundation to which by all appearances the whole imperial church could agree, despite its inner diversity (with the exception of 'unteachable' bishops such as Athanasius). Constantius had now brought about something over which his father Constantine the Great had ultimately failed: the unity of the imperial church.

However, the emperor could not enjoy his success for long. In February 360 his cousin Julian rebelled in distant Gaul; on his campaign against the usurper the emperor died unexpectedly in Tarsus in November 361. Constantius had had no time to test the durability of the Homoean church peace (which had really only swept the disputed theological questions under the table) and to safeguard it; under the short reign of his successor Julian (361–63) circumstances changed fundamentally.

CHAPTER 11

The Assembling of
the Neo-Nicenes

Emperor Julian had had a Christian upbringing, but – fascinated by Neo-Platonic philosophy, Graeco-Roman religion
and the classical culture of antiquity – long before his
accession he had secretly turned away from Christianity.
Unlike his predecessors, as sole ruler he now did not seek to
ground the unity of the empire on the unity of the Christian
church (which in the meantime he had come to despise) but
to safeguard it by the restoration of the pagan state cult.

The Homoean church peace which had been settled
shortly beforehand did not fit this plan, and Emperor Julian
sought actively to undermine it. He allowed the bishops
who had been deposed and banished under Constantius
to return to their sees, where other (Homoean) bishops
had already been installed. This 'tolerant' measure was in
reality precisely calculated: in view of the 'proven' delight of
the Christians in disputes, Julian thought it certain that the
splits in the church which had been laboriously concealed
would be renewed and hardened, and thus Christianity
would hasten its own downfall.

The banished bishops who were recalled in 362 included
Athanasius, the symbolic figure of the controversies over
Arianism. It was to his advantage that the anti-bishop
George, who had enforced the Homoean church policy,

had been lynched by a mob in Alexandria at the end of 361 – Athanasius thus had no serious rival in his episcopal city.

Contrary to what Emperor Julian perhaps expected, Athanasius did not hurl himself without restraint into theological agitation, but implemented his strategy afresh with great sensitivity. He was guided by the insight that he must not put excessive obstacles in the way of the countless bishops who had more or less willingly bowed to Constantius's religious policy if he wanted to win them over. Had all the bishops who had consented to the Homoean compromise been condemned, they would all have been made enemies. Therefore Athanasius laid down only a few elementary conditions that his fellow bishops had to fulfil to be accepted into church communion. They were to accept the Nicene Creed and reject Arianism; everything else would then be forgiven and forgotten. Pope Liberius also acted in a similar way in Rome; however, in his case such gentleness was particularly appropriate, because through his weakness towards Constantius he had compromised himself and had to hope for indulgence. But this concession was particularly brilliant on the part of Athanasius, who had always remained unyielding and had no reason for self-criticism.

Athanasius also took the next important step towards the consolidation of the Nicene faith. In February 362 he assembled a small synod which not only confirmed his own theology but was also to sound out possibilities of accepting other theological groups into church communion. These included in particular the various parties of the important metropolis of Antioch in Syria. Alongside the community of the Homoean bishop Euzoius (Arius's former deacon), with whom there could be no question of an understanding from the start, there was an Old Nicene community there around the presbyter Paulinus. Athanasius felt particularly close to it theologically, for like him this group identified the one divine substance with the one hypostasis of God. However, the community around Bishop Meletius was numerically the stronger. In December 360, with the assent of Emperor Constantius, Meletius had been elevated to the throne of Antioch, but had been replaced hardly a month later by

Euzoius – evidently because he did not fulfil the expectations of the dominant Homoean clique. However, his adherents remained loyal to him and now again gathered round him. Theologically, the Meletians advocated the Eastern doctrine of three divine hypostases, but they were very much more moderate in their subordinationism than Euzoius and his adherents.

Both groups, the Old Nicenes around Paulinus and the adherents of Meletius, now sent representatives to Alexandria. Here Athanasius named as conditions for church communion the condemnation of Arianism, the recognition of the Nicene Creed and in addition the condemnation of the doctrine that the Holy Spirit was a creature and separate from the substance (the *ousia*) of Christ. Whereas these demands did not represent a problem for the Old Nicenes, Athanasius took a further step towards the Meletians: he was aware that he had to give up the credal text of the Western synod of Serdica in 342 because in it, under the influence of Marcellus of Ancyra, the Nicene Creed had been interpreted decisively in terms of the one-hypostasis theology. Athanasius had in fact contributed to this statement in 342, but from the perspective of the year 362 it represented an insuperable obstacle to an understanding with the Meletians in Antioch. So the Bishop of Alexandria now made an effort to play down the credal text of Serdica. He said that it had been a completely superfluous explanation of the Nicene Creed and therefore was not binding. All that was binding was the faith that had been formulated in the Nicene Creed itself. Thus Athanasius also distanced himself from his former ally Marcellus of Ancyra, the bogey-man of all Eastern theologians; the close connection between the two had long been loosened, but in the present situation Marcellus was only a burden on Athanasius's aims in church politics.

However, the concern for theological consensus went even further. Athanasius asked the Meletians in what sense they would confess Father, Son and Spirit as three hypostases: would this mean that these hypostases were different in substance or separate from one another, like three human beings; that they were to be understood as different substances (Greek *ousiai*) like gold, silver and bronze, or as three principles (*archai*) or three Gods? The Meletians rejected all these possibilities, pointing out that with their doctrine they merely wanted to express faith in a holy triad, not a nominal but a real and really existing triad. For them, too, there was only one Godhead and one principle (*arche*); the Son was of the same substance as the Father (*homoousios*), and the Spirit was neither creature nor alien (to the deity). Athanasius accepted their explanations. Conversely, he asked the representatives of the Old Nicenes whether their theology of the one divine hypostasis could not be understood as Sabellius understood it (i.e. modalistically). The Old Nicenes rejected this and declared that they would speak of one hypostasis only because the Son had being from the substance of the Father and the nature (*physis*) of the two was one and the same. In conclusion, both groups once again asserted that the faith was formulated much more aptly and succinctly in the Nicene Creed and that in future they should be content with it.

The course of the negotiations indicates why Athanasius saw the Nicene Creed as a real opportunity for church unity. This creed (unlike later creeds in East and West) had never spoken explicitly of *one* divine hypostasis, nor had it spoken of *three*. What could be regarded as a logical defect from a systematic perspective proved after the event to be an advantage; precisely because the Nicene Creed had left open the question of hypostases, it could now serve as a basis for understanding.

The negotiations in Alexandria in 362, the result of which were set down in writing (in the so-called *Tome to the Antiochenes*), may be regarded as a great moment in church history, for here there was no reciprocal demarcation and polemic nor a cheap compromise (as in the Homoean imperial dogma) but an understanding of the concerns of the other party and a clarification of terminological differences. None of the groups taking part had to give up their own position (for example, Athanasius never spoke of three hypostases, even later); instead of this, the orthodox content of the different theologies was established. Here one might almost recognize a consensual ecumenical conversation in the modern sense.

However, the theological consensus did not (immediately) work out – as happens in the ecumenical world today. A hot-headed bishop from Sardinia, Lucifer of Calaris, succeeded in thwarting the efforts at reconciliation. Lucifer, who because of his opposition to Constantius II had been banished to the Thebaid in Egypt, did not take part in the negotiations in Alexandria in 362 but travelled to Antioch and there consecrated the presbyter Paulinus bishop of the Old Nicene community all by himself. This affront annoyed Bishop Meletius, who claimed to be leader of the Christians of Antioch. Therefore he did not ratify church communion with Athanasius but postponed it. By contrast, the newly-consecrated Paulinus immediately signed the *Tome to the Antiochenes* and was thereupon recognized by Athanasius as Bishop of Antioch. The schism, which seemed to have been overcome theologically, lasted for more than four decades because of the rivalry of the two bishops.

Athanasius, too, suffered a setback: his efforts at church harmony and his success in converting the pagans in Alexandria embittered Emperor Julian – the recall of the bishop had been a tactical mistake. That very year, 362, Athanasius was banished for a fourth time and again went underground. However, the following year Julian lost his life in a campaign against the Persians. With General Jovian, again a Christian assumed rule.

Athanasius immediately made contact with the new emperor Jovian by letter and travelled to Antioch from his hiding place in Egypt; there he assumed church communion with the Old Nicene Paulinus (but not with Meletius). Athanasius presented to Jovian the Nicene Creed as his confession of faith and was recognized as the legitimate Bishop of Alexandria. Other groups also attempted to win the emperor to their side and at the same time to eject their theological opponents. But Jovian was not prepared to hitch himself to the wagon of one of the parties and to give help to their church policy. He responded with clear disapproval to the suggestion that this or that bishop should be deposed and sent into exile; the whole dispute would only introduce dangerous unrest into church and empire. Thus under Jovian, too, the preservation or restoration of church peace remained the most important aim of the imperial policy on religion.

In Antioch, Bishop Meletius was able to take advantage of the hour: he assembled a synod of Syrian and Palestinian bishops who composed a credal text destined for the emperor (handed down in Socrates, *Church History* III 25.10–18) which accepted the Nicene Creed as an expression of the true and orthodox faith. The bishops, all of whom came from the Eastern, i.e. anti-Nicene, tradition, sought to make their change to the new course plausible: they explicitly agreed to the Nicene *homoousios* which indicated that Father and Son were of the same substance; the explanation stated that this term seemed inappropriate to some people but that the fathers had found a reliable explanation. It meant that the Son was begotten from the substance of the Father and was like or similar to the Father in substance (Greek *homoios kat'ousian*). The fathers would speak of the substance (the *ousia*) of God only in order to refute the godless teaching of Arius, according to which Christ came out of nothing. But the Anhomoeans would now more shamelessly preach precisely this doctrine, to the damage of church harmony.

The motivation of the Eastern bishops in attaching themselves to the Nicene Creed is obvious: it was the danger of Arianism, which had flared up again, that drove the moderate Eastern theologians into the Nicene camp. In this way it was confirmed again that the majority of the theologians of the East were not Arians, nor did they want to be.

However, what is remarkable about the synodical document is the interpretation of the Nicene *homoousios*, which had defined that Father and Son were of the same substance: *de facto* it is here identified with the Homoeousian formula *homoios kat'ousian*. In purely philological terms that is possible, since the difference in meaning between the Greek adjectives *homos* and *homoios* is not very great. However, the question remains whether the text is speaking of *one* identical divine substance (one *ousia*) or *two* which are totally like each other. So far the dispute between East and West had been over precisely that. And on this point the Meletians, too, did not express themselves precisely – the openness of the Nicene Creed to different interpretations gave them this possibility.

Promising though these beginnings were, they were thwarted by current political developments: surprisingly, Emperor Jovian died in 364 and was succeeded by the brothers Valentinian and Valens, who divided the West and the East of the empire between them. Whereas Valentinian largely practised toleration in the West, Valens in the East returned to the religious policy of the Emperor Constantius – only a few years had passed since his death at the end of 361.

In 365, Emperor Valens restored the Homoean imperial dogma. At the same time he ruled that all deposed bishops whom Emperor Julian had allowed to return were to go into exile again. Thus the status quo of the year 361 was to be restored. However, Valens did not have the prestige and the determination of Emperor Constantine and his son Constantius – for example, he had to allow Athanasius to return to Alexandria as early as 366 for fear of disturbances in Egypt. From now on the bishop could guide the fortunes of the Egyptian church almost untroubled until his death in 373.

And it was only at the beginning of the 370s that Emperor Valens could also send Bishop Meletius of Antioch into exile for a longer period. However, his community was held together by brave presbyters, and outside Antioch, too, groups assembled which had recently become open to the Nicene Creed. Three theologians are important in this connection, who because of their origin are called 'the three Cappadocians', namely Basil of Caesarea, his younger brother Gregory of Nyssa and their friend Gregory of Nazianzus. They above all achieved the real breakthrough to a conception of the theology of the Trinity which would point the way to the future and ultimately prove able to overcome the dispute over Arianism.

The pioneer work was done by the oldest of them, Basil the Great, who was consecrated bishop of the provincial capital of Caesarea in Cappadocia in 369 or 370. The crux of the theology of the Trinity had at all times been the need to give adequate expression to unity and trinity in God – now Basil succeeded in doing justice to this demand through a differentiation of concepts: hitherto both supporters and opponents of the Nicene Creed had used the terms 'hypostasis' and 'substance' (*ousia*) as corresponding to each other. The West and the Old Nicenes around Athanasius of Alexandria had always started from *one* divine substance and at the same time *one* divine hypostasis (i.e. one existing divine reality) in order to safeguard monotheism. Conversely, the East had spoken of *three* divine hypostases (three existing realities) and given each of the three hypostases its own being, its own *ousia* as individual substance, however like or similar these individual substances might be thought to be. Only in this way did the real existence or 'reality' of Father, Son and Spirit seem to be guaranteed.

The mutual correspondence of the two terms 'substance' and 'hypostasis' was originally also customary for Basil, who by origin belonged to the Homoeousian camp, which assumed two substances that were completely like each other for the two hypostases of God the Father and God the Son. However, in the controversy with the radical Arian Anhomoeans Basil learned to keep the two concepts apart.

As we know, the Anhomoeans around Aetius and Eunomius had taught that the substance (the *ousia*) of the Father was grasped precisely with the concept of unbegottenness. By contrast, the substance of the Son was not unbegottenness but begottenness and thus was totally dissimilar (Greek *anhomoios*) to the substance of the Father. According to Basil this supposedly conclusive proof began from false premises; for there is no term which could adequately describe the substance of God. If we call God the Father 'unbegotten' (or 'immortal' or 'incorruptible' or even 'good' and 'just'), with these terms we are expressing *how* God is but not *what* he is in his substance; we are forming a certain notion of God, but have not exhaustively grasped his *substance*. In truth the substance of God is inaccessible and incomprehensible to all creatures, human beings and even the angels – it is knowable only for the Father, the Son and the Holy Spirit. The assertion of the Neo-Arians around Aetius and Eunomius that they could *grasp the substance* of the Father and the Son and describe it with a *precise concept* represents a great overestimation of themselves and serves only to lead believers astray.

What more, then, do the terms 'unbegottenness' and 'begottenness' say about God the Father and God the Son? According to Basil, these terms do not relate to the divine substance, which cannot be grasped, but to the Father as Father and the Son as Son – in other words, they refer to the particular hypostasis (the distinctive reality of the Father and that of the Son). The *hypostasis* of the Father is characterized by being unbegotten and possessing the divine substance of itself. Conversely, the *hypostasis* of the Son is characterized by being begotten and possessing the same divine substance because that is communicated to it by the Father. Being unbegotten and being begotten are accordingly statements about a particular hypostasis, but not about the divine substance which underlies the hypostases. Accordingly the two terms 'substance' and 'hypostasis' can no longer be used interchangeably; they are to be kept apart and have two different meanings. The term 'substance' relates to what is common to Father and Son, what is *general*, whereas the term 'hypostasis' denotes what is *particular* to Father and Son, i.e. what makes the Father *the Father* and the Son *the Son*.

Thus in principle the Neo-Nicene solution was found. There is only *one* incomprehensible divine substance which is realized in different ways in the *three* hypostases of the Godhead (Greek *mia ousia – treis hypostaseis*): the Father possesses the divine substance *without cause* from himself, the Son *by being begotten from the Father* and the Spirit *by proceeding from the Father* (as Gregory of Nazianzus spells out clearly with John 15.26). The *what* of the divine substance, the divine nature, is the same in the case of Father, Son and Spirit, but *how* these three possess the same divine substance differs. Only through this are the three hypostases of the Godhead constituted as such; in any other respect they correspond absolutely: in their power and glory, greatness, goodness, eternity, incomprehensibility and so on. Within the Trinity there is no earlier or later, no more or less, no greater or smaller, no higher and lower. The only difference between the three divine *hypostases* (but not concerning their substance) is the unbegottenness of the Father, the begottenness of the Son and the procession of the Spirit from the Father. But by 'begetting' and 'procession' the Son and Spirit are eternally bound up with the Father, so a separation of the three hypostases cannot be imagined.

For Basil this solution came closely into view from 363/364 onwards when he wrote his books against the Anhomoean Eunomius. In the following years up to his death in 378 he further developed the Neo-Nicene conception and was supported in this by his brother Gregory of Nyssa and his scholar friend Gregory of Nazianzus, who continued the task after Basil's death.

One thing above all is noteworthy about this theology: over against the positivistic and rationalistic approach of the Anhomoeans, which was stamped by a self-confident trust in the power of human knowledge, the Cappadocians asserted the scope of human reason very much more cautiously by declaring that the divine substance was in principle incomprehensible to a created mind. Here they put themselves in the tradition of negative (or apophatic) theology, which attempts with the help of such negations to evoke an impression of the indescribable greatness of God.

According to the Cappadocians, all human notions of God remain inadequate. We attribute particular properties to God, such as goodness, justice, power, etc., but there are no limits in God and these properties are measureless: God is *infinitely* good, righteous and powerful. In reality, all the positive notions of the divine extend into the infinite and therefore a finite mind ultimately cannot understand them. But because God is in every conceivable respect infinite and boundless, there can be no distinctions within the Trinity, no more or less. If the divine as such is *infinitely* good and powerful, the Son cannot be rather less good than the Father and the Father cannot be a bit more powerful than the Son. So the subordinationist notion of an order of rank within the Trinity is excluded. There is no rank in the infinite. The only 'remnant' of such a gradated conception is to be recognized in the distinction of the three divine hypostases, since only the Father is uncaused, whereas Son and Spirit have their cause in the Father. However, this causation is thought of as being totally timeless; it has nothing to do with a temporal sequence but rather has to be understood strictly onto-*logically*. For the divine substance is eternal, and there can be no earlier or later in the eternal. Moreover the distinction between Creator and creature lies precisely here: the divine knows no extension in time which could be divided or measured, whereas the creature 'extends' within time, has beginning and duration.

Thus the theology of the Cappadocians sketches out a new order of being. The divisive ontological gulf no longer separates – as it does with Arius – the only true God (the Father), who alone is uncaused and unbegotten, from all other beings (including Son and Spirit) which are begotten, created and have come into being (in whatever way). Rather, the ontological gulf lies between the eternal, infinite and incomprehensible divine substance, which is realized in the three divine hypostases, and all that is created, temporal, finite and limited and therefore can also be known and grasped.

However, the theological creativity of the Cappadocians must not disguise the fact that the church political scene for the present gave them virtually no opportunities to help their theology of the Trinity break through. For in the East Emperor Valens persistently attempted (though with changing emphasis and success) to impose the Homoean imperial dogma and to shut out the theological opposition. The situation was so difficult that the bishops of the East who wanted to recognize the Nicene Creed as the basis for the unity of the church had to attempt to close ranks with the West.

In 366 a delegation of three bishops was sent to Rome to gain the support of Pope Liberius. The pope initially refused to receive them because he thought that they were Arians. The bishops refuted this prejudice and declared that they would confess the Nicene *homoousios*, which designated the similarity or likeness between Father and Son in substance (according to another tradition: in every respect) and was to be understood in an anti-Arian way. They were then given a hearing. The delegation formally assented to the Council of Nicaea and presented the Nicene Creed in writing. At the same time it condemned the heretical parties, on the one hand the Anomoeans who represented radical Neo-Arianism, and on the other Marcellus of Ancyra and his disciple Photinus, whom they regarded as modalists. Pope Liberius accepted this declaration and gave the bishops a letter to take home with them to the East which would seal church communion. Here it is remarkable that for the first time in decades a bridge, however narrow, had been built between East and West and that here a Roman bishop accepted the condemnation of Marcellus of Ancyra which had so long burdened relations between East and West. That meant a change of course which acted as a signal.

However, this successful contact was again lost after the delegation returned to the East, because disputes again broke out there. Moreover Pope Liberius died in 366 and his successor Damasus was made of sterner stuff than his predecessor.

Pope Damasus again put the alliance between Rome and Athanasius of Alexandria in the foreground. In 372 he sent a deacon to Alexandria who was to deliver a Roman synodical letter (the letter *Confidimus quidem* which is attested in *Codex Veronensis* LX) to the catholic bishops of the East; in it the Homoean imperial dogma was condemned and the Nicene Creed was required as the basis of faith. Moreover the Roman synod confessed in respect of Father, Son and Spirit one Godhead (*deitas*), one power (*virtus*), one figure (*figura*) and one substance (*substantia*). From Alexandria the papal delegate travelled on to Cappadocia to gain the assent of the Eastern bishops to the Roman text.

The bishops reacted uncertainly. They felt that the Roman

letter was an attempt to impose the traditional Western view of the divine unity also on the East, on the basis of the Nicene Creed: hadn't the phrase *una substantia* to be referred to the doctrine of the one divine hypostasis? And what was one to imagine by the *one* figure of the Godhead (*una figura*)? On the basis of such reservations the bishops around Meletius of Antioch gave only a cautious response to the Roman synodical letter in a pro-Nicene direction without mentioning the term hypostasis, but at the same time asked for effective support from the West (cf. among the letters of Basil of Caesarea, *Letter* 92).

That did not satisfy Pope Damasus. He required of the Eastern bishops a verbal repetition of the Roman synodical letter as a confirmation of their faith, and this inevitably seemed to them to be intolerable arrogance. Only Paulinus of Antioch, who as bishop still led the small Old Nicene community of his city and had no difficulties with the Roman standpoint, acceded to the pope's demand and was thereupon accepted into church communion by Damasus in 375 – an understandable step, but a great mistake in church politics, since Paulinus and his small community in the East were largely isolated.

However, contacts between the East and Rome were not completely broken off. The tense church–political situation was the occasion for further calls for help for the Eastern bishops, who felt that they had been left in the lurch in their fight against the church policy of the Homoean Emperor Valens. Pope Damasus responded with a letter (of which the fragment *Ea gratia* is preserved in *Codex Veronensis* LX) which shows that the exchange of delegations had after all promoted mutual understanding. Here Damasus speaks in respect of the Trinity of *one* force (*virtus*), *one* majesty (*maiestas*), *one* Godhead (*divinitas*) and *one* indivisible power (*potestas*), but no longer of *one substantia* and *figura*. Instead of this, strikingly he uses a Greek loanword: he confesses *one ousia* [*sic!*] of the Trinity, and moreover three everlasting persons (*tres personae*) – this change of diction represented a concession to the East. People in Rome had seen that the expression *una substantia* could be misunderstood in the

East and moreover the divine Trinity also had to be conceptualized.

In a further letter to the Eastern bishops (the central statements of which are preserved in the fragment *Non nobis quidquam* in *Codex Veronensis* LX) the pope again made it known that he wanted to take account of the terminological sensitivity of the East. The letter speaks of the *trinitas coaeternae et unius essentiae*, of the Trinity of one essence which is co-eternal and unique. This time the papal letter does not use the old Western watchword *una substantia*, nor the Greek loanword *ousia*, but the Latin expression *una essentia*. This made it clear that Rome did not want to lay down the Old Nicene doctrine of the *one* hypostasis, but accepted the Neo-Nicene doctrine of *one* divine *ousia*, for *essentia* is etymologically the appropriate equivalent of the Greek term *ousia*. In this way the East had Roman documents in its hands on which the basis of a union seemed possible.

In the West the pope's concern to consolidate the church on a Nicene line went further. In 378 and 382 Damascus convened synods in Rome at which a famous text, the so-called *Tome of Damasus*, was composed and developed. This was a confession for the synod of Nicaea and a listing of numerous errors in the doctrine of the Trinity which should safeguard the orthodox line against deviations. If we sum up these demarcations, the following picture results: Father, Son and Spirit possess *one* power (*potestas*) and *one* substance (*substantia*) – the current Latin term occurs again here, as this is a definition of the Western position. And as confirmation it is said that there is only *one* Godhead, *one* power, majesty and mightiness, only *one* glory, dominion and reign, only *one* divine will and *one* truth. All these terms are meant to emphasize the oneness of God and thus clearly express monotheism, which had always been the concern of the West. But at the same time the Sabellian error, according to which Father and Son are one and the same, is condemned. The view that the Son of God is a 'spreading' of the Father or without substance, and will have an end, is also rejected. These clarifications are directed against the teaching of Marcellus of Ancyra, with whom Rome had still been in communion forty years earlier. In addition, the *Tome of Damasus* teaches that there are three true persons (*tres personae verae*) of the Father and the Son and the Holy Spirit. Here, too, we can again detect an effort to take account of the problems of the East, for the talk is not just of three persons but of three *true* persons; that is meant to express their real existence, their reality, and in principle coincides with the Eastern term hypostases. Of course the *Tome of Damasus* also condemns Arius and his Anomoean successors, but that is only to be expected in a Western document.

All in all, the *Tome of Damasus* successfully sums up the state of theological discussion in the West and indicates a similar stage of reflection to that attained by the three Cappadocians in the East. Theological union seemed tangibly close, yet the decisive impulse again came from the political side.

In 378 the Homoean emperor Valens was killed in the war against the Goths. To protect the frontier of the empire, Gratian (the son of the deceased Valentinian), the Augustus of the West, sent the Spanish general Theodosius to the crisis area as *magister militum* and after initial successes in January 379 named him the Augustus of the East. The thirty-two-year-old Theodosius had grown up in the West; he was not yet baptized, but inwardly already firmly committed to Christianity, that is, to the Western Christianity loyal to Nicaea. Like his predecessors, this emperor too was convinced that the unity of the empire had to be safeguarded on a religious basis. Now he saw the foundation of religious unity not in the Homoean imperial dogma which – apart from the years 361–64 – had been official doctrine in the East for almost twenty years, but made a change in course. Even before his baptism in autumn 380, on 28 February of the same year the emperor issued an edict which was initially addressed to the Eastern capital, Constantinople, but was soon seen as a programmatic manifesto, the famous edict *Cunctos populos* (*Codex Theodosianus* XVI 1.2). It ordained that all subjects of the emperor should follow the religion of the apostle Peter which he had handed down to the

Romans. The Roman pontiff Damasus and the Alexandrian bishop Peter (Athanasius's successor) would confess this faith. Belief was to be in *one* Godhead of the Father, the Son and the Holy Spirit under the concept of equal majesty and holy Trinity. Anyone who did not observe this law would bear the shame of heretical doctrine and was threatened with punishment from God and the emperor.

So here the confession of the bishops of Rome and Alexandria, who both stood in the Nicene tradition, is elevated to the norm of faith. In content this norm of faith is described rather vaguely – at any rate there is talk of the one Godhead and the holy Trinity. The imperial edict is no more precise. Instead, it refers to the bishops named as guarantors of the norm of faith: they are to provide the orientation. In the West that was no problem, but how were things in the church of the East?

There, after the death of Valens in 378, Bishop Meletius of Antioch had returned to his episcopal see and in 379 had convened a large synod of more than 150 Neo-Nicene bishops. This synod had endorsed a compilation of Roman letters which had reached the East, all of which put forward the Nicene faith. It comprised letters of Pope Damasus from past years which have already been mentioned. The members of the synod signed these texts in Antioch and sent them to Rome, as Pope Damasus had required. This was to document their agreement in the faith. However, the final reconciliation with Rome did not come about, since the Pope stood by the Old Nicene Paulinus as the legitimate Bishop of Antioch. Nevertheless, the expectations which the new emperor had expressed to his subjects in the East had already been fulfilled by the Meletians in their confirmation of the letters of Damasus.

Emperor Theodosius showed greater breadth of vision in church politics than Pope Damasus. It was clear to him that the unity of the church could be produced only on a broad and reliable basis. Therefore the emperor did not support the insignificant Paulinus, who had hardly any adherents outside Antioch, but Meletius, who had recently gathered 150 bishops around him and put forward the Neo-Nicene theology which was also acceptable in the West. Therefore it was to Meletius that the emperor entrusted the preparation of a new council in Constantinople which was to seal the success of Neo-Nicene theology in the East.

At this council the question of the Holy Spirit was also to be resolved. For a long time it had led a shadowy existence in the discussion of the theology of the Trinity, but in recent years it had been brought into the foreground.

CHAPTER 12

The Question of the Holy Spirit

For a long period, the controversy about the Christian image of God had concentrated on the debate concerning how the relationship between God the Father and the pre-existent Son of God (the Logos) was to be defined. By contrast there was far less reflection on the status of the Holy Spirit, although from the beginning of course the Spirit was of great importance for the faith, for liturgy and piety of Christians (one need only think of the phenomenon of inspired prophecy in the early church or Christian martyrdom, which could be endured only 'in the power of the Spirit'). The fact that the equivalent for 'spirit' in Greek is neuter (*to pneuma*) and thus evokes more the idea of a gift than that of a subject, and that talk of the Pneuma – unlike talk of the Son of God – did not immediately and automatically pose a question to monotheism must also have played a role in bracketing off the Spirit from the discussion. Moreover Judaism had already been able to speak quite unproblematically of the spirit (*ruah*) of God without seeing the unity of Yahweh being affected.

Note had always been taken of the Spirit in the sketches of the Christian image of God, because he was mentioned together with Father and Son in the biblical tradition (e.g. in the scene of the baptism of Jesus in the Jordan, in the baptismal command in Matt. 28.19 or in Paul's closing greeting in 2 Cor. 13.13). At the end of the second century

117

Irenaeus of Lyons had spoken metaphorically of the Son and the Spirit in the perspective of the economy of salvation as the 'two hands' of God. At the beginning of the third century Tertullian of Carthage had defined the *spiritus sanctus* in the course of prosopological exegesis (which enquires into who the 'speaker' is in biblical verses) as a particular *persona* and given him the titles *deus* and *dominus* as a consequence of his doctrine of the Trinity. A little later, Origen of Alexandria had developed the beginnings of an explicit pneumatology by defining the Spirit in his work *On First Principles* as a distinct hypostasis (cf. I 1.3) and alongside the tradition of faith had also formulated open questions about the Spirit, for example whether the Holy Spirit had been originated or not, and whether he himself was also to be regarded as 'Son of God' (*Preface* 4).

All in all, however, the Spirit had never been brought into the centre of the disputes – even the Nicene Creed (325) had limited itself in its third article to the formula: 'We believe ... in the Holy Spirit.' For Arius and his followers and up to the Neo-Arians, however, there could be no doubt: if even the Logos/Son is to be regarded only as 'perfect creature', and moreover the only one to be created directly by the Father, the Holy Spirit is yet more at the level of the (other) creatures who have come into being through the Logos. The moderate Subordinationists emphasized – for example in the second Antiochene formula of 341 – only that the rank of the three hypostases and the gradation of their glory was indicated precisely by the enumeration of the Trinity in the baptismal command of the risen Christ (Matt. 28.19). Moreover numerous credal texts limited themselves to taking up New Testament statements about the Holy Spirit which could not easily be disputed (thus still the fourth formula of Sirmium from 359 and the Homoean imperial dogma of 359/60).

The pneumatological discussion took on a dynamic of its own only through the Homoeousians, who with reference to the 'begetting' of the Son taught the likeness/similarity of Father and Son in substance – but what did that mean in respect of the Holy Spirit? Was the Holy Spirit to be said to be 'begotten', like the Son? But in that case the Son would no longer be the 'only-begotten' or the 'only' one, and there would be *two* Sons! If, on the other hand, the Spirit was unbegotten like the Father, one had to assume *two* unbegottens and that would mean *two* Gods. And if the Spirit was derived from the Son, at the same time the Father would be 'grandfather' of the Spirit – absurd speculations!

Whereas some of the Homoeousians documented their own perplexity in the face of this aporia (which had come about through the fixation on the 'Father–Son' scheme) and retreated to the position that the Pneuma was to be designated neither God nor creature, others drew a more radical consequence: they firmly defined the Spirit as creature. To support this thesis they referred to statements such as John 1.3, 'All things [including the Spirit] were made by the Logos' or the words of God in Amos 4.13 LXX: 'I am he who ... creates Spirit and proclaims his Christ among men.' They concluded from the triadic formula in 1 Tim. 5.21 ('I beseech you before God, Jesus Christ and the elect angels') that the Spirit must be the highest of the angels mentioned and called him a 'serving being' (with reference to Heb. 1.14, where the angels are called 'serving *pneumata*').

These theses were presented in the 350s, when the Homoeousians were marshalling themselves against the Anhomoeans. Athanasius, who in 356 had gone underground in the Egyptian desert, fleeing the persecution of Emperor Constantius, had news of this through Bishop Serapion of Thmuis in the Nile delta. He was one of the first to develop orthodox pneumatology in the letters that he wrote in reply (and then required this pneumatology at the Synod of Alexandria in 362).

Athanasius argues first with formal logic: the Holy Trinity (Greek *trias* – a term long current and recognized in early Christian theology) would not be a true triad if in it Creator (namely Father and Son) and creature (viz. the Spirit) were bundled together. In that case one would more consistently have to speak of a divine duality (*dyas*) on the one hand and of creation on the other. So the unity of the divine substance may not be split in the Holy Triad. Secondly, Athanasius presents hermeneutical principles for dealing with the Bible: it must be recognized that the Holy Spirit is not designated everywhere that the term *pneuma* (breeze, wind, breath, spirit) occurs. In biblical verses it has to be indicated specifically whether the *Holy* Spirit is being designated (that is not the case in Amos 4.13). Furthermore, the reference of the elect angels in 1 Tim. 5.21 to the Holy Spirit is forced and therefore inadmissible, even if this interpretation is grounded with the help of biblical 'figures of speech' (Greek *tropoi*, so that Athanasius brands his opponents *tropikoi*).

But Athanasius's most important argument is orientated on salvation history and soteriology. From the creation onwards (cf. Ps. 32.6 LXX) the Spirit has taken part in the divine plan of salvation: he inspired the prophets, co-operated in the incarnation of the Logos (cf. Luke 1.35), filled the apostles and hallows believers. Without the Spirit, baptism is incomplete and ineffective – how then can the Spirit be a creature? Can a creature save and perfect human beings? For Athanasius that is inconceivable and from it he draws the conclusion (in *Letter to Serapion* 1.27) that the one Pneuma is proper to and of the same substance (*homoousion*) as the *one* Logos and the *one* God – in this way the Nicene concept of consubstantiality (*homoousia*) is also extended to the Spirit (we find the same concept in the Alexandrian theologian Didymus the Blind, who possibly wrote his pneumatological treatise *On the Holy Spirit* likewise before 362; according to others it was composed only after 370; cf. *Holy Spirit* 17.81; 32.145).

By contrast the Neo-Nicene Basil of Caesarea expresses himself far more cautiously in his great work *On the Holy Spirit*. Here it should be noted that the Cappadocian came from the Homoeousian camp and had to grapple much more intensively with this area than the Old Nicene Athanasius, for whom the *homoousia* of the (whole) divine *trias* could not be a problem. Basil's situation was quite different: because of the pneumatological disputes around 373 he even broke off the friendship with one of his companions and spiritual teachers, Eustathius of Sebaste. Discussions with him shape the treatise on the Holy Spirit which Basil completed around

374 or 375 to dissuade the Pneumatomachi ('fighters against the Spirit') from their position. That explains why the author avoids excessively provocative statements and does not forthrightly call the Holy Spirit 'God' or emphasize that the Spirit is consubstantial with the Father and the Son.

Instead of this, Basil emphasizes the equality of rank within the Trinity, as it is clearly expressed in the command of the risen Christ to baptize in the name of the Father *and* of the Son *and* of the Holy Spirit (cf. Matt. 28.19, *Holy Spirit* 10.24–26). Unlike the Eastern subordinationists, Basil thus sees Matt. 28.19 as documenting, not a gradated order of ranks, but the equality of Father, Son and Spirit. Their communion follows from the same activity in salvation history, at creation, in the time of the Old Testament, at the sending of Jesus, the founding of the church and even in the judgement, in which the fullness of the Spirit will represent the reward, and the loss of the Spirit one of the punishments (cf. *Holy Spirit* 16.37–40). Like the Father and the Son, the Spirit too gives life (Basil quotes John 6.63 in *Holy Spirit* 24.56). And the Spirit is rightly called 'Lord' in the New Testament like the Father and the Son (the cryptic passage 2 Cor. 3.17 is cited as proof in *Holy Spirit* 21.52). According to Wisdom 1.7 LXX, the Spirit of the Lord fills the earth, so his greatness has no limit, i.e. he is 'by nature divine' – this is the clearest reference to the divinity of the Holy Spirit in Basil's work (*Holy Spirit* 23.54). The Bishop of Caesarea energetically argues that the Spirit is to be glorified *with* the Father and the Son – in worship the Spirit is not to be separated from the Father and the Son (cf. *Holy Spirit* 23.54–26.64). By contrast, in the older doxological tradition glory was shown to the Father *through* the Son *in* the Holy Spirit – a linguistic rule on the precision of which the Pneumatomachi insisted, because they thought that in it the gradation within the Trinity is reproduced with theological exactitude.

By contrast, for Basil there was no question of any kind of subordination of the Spirit to God the Father and the Son. On the other hand, in the situation of the time around 374/375, which was difficult for Asia Minor (Emperor Valens was still promoting his Homoean church policy, whereas the

Eastern bishops were at odds with one another), the divinity of the Holy Spirit could not be taught more clearly than Basil attempted in his treatise. How wise this restraint was, was to be shown at the Council of Constantinople in 381, which in its doctrine of the Spirit largely followed the model of the Bishop of Caesarea. Basil himself was not to see this success, as he died at the end of 378, before the accession of Emperor Theodosius.

CHAPTER 13

The Council of Constantinople and the Agreement with the West

Emperor Theodosius must have pursued the plan to consolidate the Eastern imperial church by a council right from his accession – this council was then summoned for May 381. This second ecumenical council in our numbering is striking in various respects. Given the participants, it was not an 'ecumenical' council but a synod of the bishops of the East (orientated on Neo-Nicene theology), in which not all regions were represented equally. The pope was not invited, nor did he send legates. Bishop Acholius of Thessalonica, who had baptized Emperor Theodosius the year before, is the only 'Western' participant known by name; moreover Macedonia had only been counted in the Western half of the empire since 380. The leadership of the assembly lay in the hands of a bishop whom Rome did not recognize, Meletius of Antioch, but he died soon after the opening of the council. The assemblies of bishops were held in a church, not in the palace of the emperor, who (by comparison with Constantine) kept entirely in the background. He did not take part personally in the deliberations, nor was he represented by officials. Acts of the council have not been handed down and the creed which was formulated in Constantinople has survived only because it was received seventy years later at the Council of Chalcedon (451) alongside the Nicene Creed as a normative text – a prime example of the immense importance that the later reception of a council has for its evaluation in church history.

The council fathers (around 150 in number) had to deal with various disputed questions, for example with the new appointment to the see of Constantinople after the Homoean bishop Demophilus had had to yield to pressure from the emperor, or with the question who would succeed Bishop Meletius in Antioch after he died in May 381. The Neo-Nicenes rejected the proposal that the Old Nicene Paulinus should now be recognized as Bishop of Antioch, and this refusal cemented the Antiochene schism for further decades.

However, what are important for us are the dogmatic discussions of the council fathers with representatives of the 'Pneumatomachi' (also called 'Macedonians' after an earlier Bishop of Constantinople), who were added to the discussions, presumably at the urging of the emperor, to complete the unity of the church. The negotiations themselves failed, but the text of the creed that the council formulated still shows the line along which attempts were made to seek agreement on the question of the Holy Spirit. This text (for the first time handed down in the acts of the Council of Chalcedon) runs:

> We believe in one God Father, Almighty, the Maker of heaven and earth, and of all things visible and invisible. And in one Lord Jesus Christ, the Son of God, only-begotten from the Father before all ages; Light from Light, true God from true God; begotten, not made, consubstantial with the Father; by whom all things were made. Who, for us men and for our salvation, came down from heaven, and became incarnate by the Holy Spirit and the virgin Mary, and was made man; was crucified also for us under Pontius Pilate; and suffered, and was buried; and the third day rose again, according to the Scriptures; and ascended into heaven, and is seated at the right hand of the Father; and will come again with glory

to judge the living and the dead; whose kingdom will have no end. And in the Holy Spirit, the Lord and Giver of Life; who proceeds from the Father; who together with the Father and the Son is worshipped and glorified; who spoke through the prophets. In one holy, catholic, and apostolic church. We confess one baptism for the remission of sins. We look for the resurrection of the dead, and the life of the coming age. Amen.

In its first and second parts the creed is largely orientated on the Nicene Creed, but a number of changes can be listed: for example the firm statement of the Nicene Creed that the Son is begotten *'from the substance of the Father'* is omitted – does the (anti-Nicene) reservation about the absurd notion of a 'divisibility' of the divine substance still have an effect here? The avoidance of the double statement that the Son is 'God from God' and 'true God from true God' seems to be merely stylistic. By contrast, the insertion that the kingdom of the risen and exalted Jesus Christ *'will have no end'* can be interpreted with some certainty as a theological rejection of the teaching of Marcellus of Ancyra. It was necessary because Marcellus had always seen himself as a defender of the Nicene Creed, and the bishops of the East wanted to maintain that their interpretation of the Nicene Creed was not coloured by him.

However, what is more important is the third, predominantly pneumatological, part of the creed, which is a new formulation by comparison with the Nicene Creed and is aimed at the Pneumatomachi. Here the divine dignity of the Holy Spirit is described with the term 'Lord' (which in Greek is put in the neuter, *to kyrion*, by analogy with *to pneuma*, something that cannot be expressed in English), and also with the Johannine statements that the Spirit gives life (John 6.63) and proceeds from the Father (John 15.26). It should be remarked in passing that here the creed keeps strictly to the New Testament wording. The statement that the Spirit proceeds from the Father *and the Son* (*filioque*) represents a later Latin insertion into the creed which even now separates the Eastern and Western churches. In the Constantinopolitan Creed the reference to the inspiration of the prophets is also to be understood as a recourse to the biblical salvation history (cf. 2 Peter 1.21). In addition, it is stated that the Pneuma is co-worshipped (Greek *symprosky-noumenon*) and co-glorified (Greek *syndoxazomenon*) with the Father and the Son. However, there is no clear reference to the *homoousia* of the Spirit with Father and Son, as had been stated for Son and Father since Nicaea. How is this 'defect' to be explained?

It seems most plausible to see the aim of the creed as analogous to that of Basil of Caesarea in composing his treatise *On the Holy Spirit*, a series of arguments from which recur here. The text can be understood as an attempt to come to an agreement with the Pneumatomachi on the basis of the Neo-Nicene doctrine of the Spirit. So the formulations must not be too provocative. Instead of proclaiming the ontological *homoousia* of the Spirit, the liturgical-doxological *homotimia* is put in the foreground: the Spirit shares the same honour (Greek *time*), worship and glorification as the Father and the Son. This indeed expresses the divinity of the Spirit, but in a more indirect way, which does not prove unsympathetic. However, this strategy did not achieve its aim: the creed remained unacceptable to the Pneumatomachi.

Scholars still argue about how the creed came into being. Does it represent a revision and expansion of the Nicene Creed, or is it (also) based on other creeds? In my view we must start from the assumption that in the 'construction' of the creed the council fathers resorted to proven material (and here that means the Nicene Creed), but where it seemed necessary they inserted their own 'building blocks': these included the short addition against Marcellus and even more the longer pneumatological passage which can be regarded as 'Basilian'.

Canon 1 which the council passed proves that the bishops still recognized the Nicene Creed as a binding formulation of faith:

> The faith of the 318 fathers who met in Nicaea in Bithynia may not be abolished but must remain in force. And any heresy shall be anathematized, and especially that of the Anomoeans and Arians [the Homoeans are meant by

the latter] ... the Semi-Arians or Pneumatomachi, the Sabellians, Marcellians and Photinians ...

Accordingly, it was the concern of the council to help the Nicene faith to break through against its Neo-Arian, Homoean and Pneumatomachian adversaries on the one hand but likewise against Marcellian 'false interpretations' on the other.

Canon 1 also condemns the adherents of Apollinaris of Laodicea. This indicates that alongside the theology of the Trinity proper, even before the council in Constantinople the question of the incarnation of the Logos had become an acute one. It was to dominate the ecumenical councils of Ephesus in 431 and Chalcedon in 451.

The council fathers also composed a dogmatic document in the form of a *Tome*, but its content has not come down to us directly; it must be inferred from a later source (see below). Before the bishops parted in July 381 they asked Emperor Theodosius to confirm the decisions made. Theodosius acceded to their wish and in addition in his edict of 30 July 381 (*Codex Theodosianus* XVI 1.3) named a series of 'norm bishops' with whom all fellow-bishops of a region had to be in communion if they were not to be driven from their churches.

With the Council of Constantinople the crisis that the theology of Arius had sparked off was overcome, at least in principle, in the east of the empire. What still had to be achieved was reconciliation with the Western churches. These likewise assembled in the late summer of 381 at a synod in Aquileia to proceed against the last Homoean bishops of the West. Ambrose of Milan played a leading role in it; he himself had been elected as successor to a Homoean in 374. The plan to assemble the churches of East and West at a great council in Rome in 382 probably came from him: the council was meant to clarify not least the disputed personal questions (in particular the West wanted to have a say in the decision over the occupation of the sees of Constantinople and Antioch). The plan for a council was transmitted to the three reigning emperors (the rulers of the West, Gratian and his younger brother Valentinian II, and Theodosius) and likewise to the bishops of the East, but understandably it was hardly popular with the latter.

As early as the summer of 382 the bishops of the eastern half of the empire again gathered in Constantinople to react to the initiative from the West. They composed a synodical letter (preserved in Theodoret, *Church History* V 9) to their fellow-bishops, who gathered in Rome, and gave a diplomatic excuse for staying away. After the tribulations under the rule of the 'Arians' (again the Homoeans are meant) they now had enough to do in consolidating their communities and could not leave them orphaned for a long period of time; therefore a journey to Rome was unthinkable. However, in order to document the mutual agreement in the theology of the Trinity the members of the synod referred to the 'very old' faith of Nicaea which accorded with Christian baptism (in the name of the Father and the Son and the Holy Spirit). They confessed faith in

> one Godhead, power and one substance (*ousia*) of the Father and of the Son and of the Holy Spirit, the dignity being the same in honour (*homotimos*) and the reign being co-eternal in three most perfect [*sic!*] hypostases or three perfect persons, so that neither the sickness of Sabellius can spread, according to which the hypostases are confused and their properties are done away with, nor can the blasphemy of the Eunomians [i.e. the Neo-Arians], the Arians [viz. Homoeans] and Pneumatomachi gain power ...

To explain this short version of the faith, the Neo-Nicene bishops of the East refer to the decisions of their synod in Antioch in 379, and also to those of the '*ecumenical synod*' of 381 – that makes a claim for this synod which only much later was also to become established in the West.

The reference to the *Tome* of 381 (which is now lost) allows us to infer its content. Alongside the confirmation of the Nicene faith and the rejection of heresies about the theology of the Trinity (see Canon 1 of the council of 381) it will have contained the Neo-Nicene confession of the *one* substance of God in *three* perfect hypostases. Here the equation of the *three* hypostases with *three* perfect persons (*prosopa*) takes note of the Western terminology but at the same time makes it clear that the *prosopa* are not to be understood as the masks or roles of actors which could promote a modalistic doctrine of God, but as *perfect* – i.e. as really existing and distinct – in the sense of the Greek hypostases theology. Conversely, the explicit identification of 'hypostases' and 'persons' signals to the West that Eastern theology did not start from *three* divine 'substances', as had long been imputed by the West because of the possibility of rendering the Greek term *hypostasis* with the Latin *substantia*. In this way dogmatic understanding between East and West seemed guaranteed.

Equally important to the members of the synod was an emphasis on the regulation in church law that church provinces (eparchies) or imperial dioceses were themselves responsible for new appointments of bishops (cf. Canon 4 of Nicaea and Canon 2 of Constantinople). This was to underline the legitimacy of the election of Nectarius as Bishop of Constantinople in 381 and the ordination of Flavian as successor to Meletius of Antioch which had taken place in the meanwhile.

In Rome the delegates from the Eastern synod were received with good will, and even church communion with Nectarius of Constantinople came about. However, the controversy over Antioch remained unresolved. Pope Damasus maintained that the Old Nicene Paulinus was the legitimate Bishop of Antioch (and his fellow-bishop in Alexandria also maintained this position). This attitude is understandable as an expression of continuity and consistency in church politics, but at the same time it shows a lack of flexibility and insight into conditions in the East, since there Paulinus continued to remain completely isolated. This unfortunate fixation on an outsider, which increasingly represented an anachronism, could only be corrected after the death of Paulinus and his immediate successor. In 394 Bishop Flavian of Antioch was finally recognized in Alexandria, and four years later also by Rome. In this way, after the theological unity, church–political unity was restored between East and West.

Nevertheless the decade-long split between the Eastern and Western churches left its traces. In Canon 3 the Council of Constantinople had claimed for the Eastern capital the pre-eminence of honour after the Bishop of Rome (and the corresponding privileges), since Constantinople was the new Rome – a definition offensive not only to Alexandria, which so far had played the most significant role alongside Rome, but also to Rome, as it was above all felt to compete with the claim of the Bishop of Rome to primacy (grounded in the apostle Peter). Thus despite the reconciliation in the dispute over the doctrine of the Trinity, new material for conflict was created – the rivalry between Rome and Constantinople was to prove a heavy burden in church history.

The church–political implementation of Neo-Nicene orthodoxy which was also practised by the state side with the help of laws against heretics still took some time, as did the literary assimilation of the theological controversy and the deepening of the doctrine of the Trinity – one need only recall the ambitious work *Against Eunomius* in which Gregory of Nyssa between 380 and 383 grappled with the theology and confession of the Anomoean Eunomius, or the fifteen books *On the Trinity* which Augustine of Hippo composed between 399 and 419. But the essential decisions had been taken, the most important directions set out. The Nicene faith was politically guaranteed by its most resolute champion, Theodosius, the Augustus of the East, who increasingly became the dominant figure on the political scene and in the years 394/395 was the last emperor to exercise sole rule over the whole empire.

Here, however, it must not be overlooked that the non-Nicene doctrine of the Trinity experienced a late hey-day among the Germanic tribes. The Goths had turned to Christianity in the time of the Emperor Constantius; under the influence of their Bishop Ulfilas they adopted the Homoean imperial dogma and handed it on to other Germanic tribes (e.g. the Vandals and Lombards), but they did not participate in the theological development under Emperor Theodosius. In the course of time these tribes settled on Roman territory. To the native Catholic population they must have seemed 'Arians' – thus in addition to the political and military opposition between the peoples the incompatibility of confessions was also a burden. It was therefore of the utmost significance for the Middle Ages that a Germanic tribe, the Franks, adopted Christianity in its catholic variant at the end of the fifth century. Whereas the other Germanic kingdoms perished (the kingdom of the Vandals in 533 and that of the Ostrogoths in Italy in 555) or their kings finally converted to Catholicism (thus in 587 the West Gothic king Reccared I and in 653 the Lombard king Aripert I), the kingdom of the catholic Franks not only survived but developed into a European power of the first order. Its most important ruler was to be Charlemagne, who in the year 800 renewed the role of emperor in the West.

CHAPTER 14

Prospect

If we now survey the course and result of the debate on the theology of the Trinity, it becomes clear that the complexity and dynamic of this process of clarification tells against the assumption that here the truth which had long since been established again imposed itself victoriously and unerringly in the face of all tribulations and disputes. What was defined as the church's doctrine of the Trinity at the ecumenical councils of Nicaea and Constantinople had first to be recognized as a question to theology and discussed, amidst much controversy, before the Neo-Nicene solution to the problem could come into view. And in view of the impenetrable theological jungle (through which in any case this account has only been able to blaze paths) we may ask: does at least the result of this laborious struggle over the Christian image of God, namely the Neo-Nicene doctrine of the *one* Godhead in *three* persons or the *one* divine substance in *three* hypostases, seem convincing to present-day observers, who are separated from the discussions of the early church by more than 1500 years? Can they recognize in it the historically mediated revelation of God?

The objections which can be made to this view seem grave. The very terminology of the Neo-Nicene doctrine must today be framed with hermeneutical explanations if it is not to be misleading; otherwise talk of the hypostases of the Godhead remains incomprehensible for most Christians and the unguarded application to the theology of the Trinity of the modern concept of person orientated on human beings would fail to do justice to the meaning of the creed of the early church – the co-eternal and indissolubly connected 'persons' of the Godhead are not to be seen in analogy to three human persons existing separately from one another.

But the historical gulf harbours yet more problems: the concept of the Logos as the mediator between transcendence and cosmos (in biblical terms the role of the Logos as mediator at creation) which was so important for early Christian discourse was plausible in the Platonic milieu of antiquity; it helped to bridge the gulf between unity and diversity, absolute transcendence and immanence, between pure intellect and the material world – but we today no longer feel the intellectual problem and stand (in amazement or perplexity) before an element in ancient philosophy which has been so to speak canonized by the history of its influence. To put it in more general terms: how far does the time-conditioned influence of ancient (and that means pagan) philosophy extend to the Christian doctrine of the Trinity, and how is it to be evaluated theologically? Conversely, what does it mean for the understanding of the Trinity if today our horizon of understanding is no longer (predominantly) shaped by Platonism?

The political interference in the theological debate is also likely to provoke scepticism: wasn't Emperor Constantine already less concerned with the quest for truth than with the unity of the empire on a religious basis? Didn't the stubborn efforts of his son Constantius to achieve a theological compromise aim at the lowest common denominator on which the parties in dispute were to agree? Wasn't it mere chance that because of a military emergency, rule in the East of the empire fell to the Spanish Theodosius, who was orientated on Nicaea, so that he had the opportunity also to realize his church–political goal there? Does the Neo-Nicene faith thus represent just a further and last variant in the power-play of theological ideas – a variant which was able to establish itself for political reasons?

And if we turn once again to the content of the debate: don't the self-confidence and the sharp (often also unjust) polemic of the opponents, the deliberate distortion and exaggeration of opposing positions, the almost sophistic pedantry and violent interpretations of difficult biblical passages, prove repulsive over wide areas? We must not note such abuses on just one side of the parties in dispute – an ideologically coloured painting in black and white will not do justice to the historical evidence.

A look at history is sobering. But at the same time it presents a challenge. In view of the problems I have mentioned, those who imagine that God's ways with human beings are all too straightforward and simple (or despair of them because they are indeed not so straightforward) are called on to break up customary religious schemes of thought and extend their own horizons so as to be able to do theological justice to reality. The *risk* of monotheism does not consist in making an arbitrary selection of reality in terms of one's own ideology, bracketing off disturbing problems and allowing only what fits, but in tracing back the complexity, the perplexing diversity and interlinking of phenomena to a last (albeit 'impenetrable') principle which is not one factor among many but the incomprehensible ground of the whole.

That the history of revelation is not played out untouched by external influence as it were in a 'vacuum' in the history of ideas is not a defect but a touchstone of the monotheistic view of the world. The philosophical systems of Middle- and Neo-Platonism or the Stoa are not simply to be dismissed as non-Christian intellectual constructions which 'had to' be overcome; rather, they are of decisive importance for the self-communication of God in the sphere of history, which is not a clean sheet, but is already shaped, and its content determined, by ideas. The legacy of ancient philosophy has entered into Christianity (likewise into Judaism, Islam and modern philosophy) – but that does not amount to 'contamination with inauthentic intellectual material'; rather, it is material for fruitful controversy which will always move between the poles of assimilation and demarcation.

It is the same with the political entanglements. Anyone who confesses the God of the Bible as the God of history must reflect how far Emperors Constantine and Constantius, no less than Theodosius or even Emperor Julian (whose tactics had quite different consequences from those he desired), have a genuine place in the historical context, which represents the matrix of the self-disclosure of God. That does not mean approving or even theologically legitimizing the imperial policy (along with its principles, its ideological claim and its forcible measures). But it does free us from a compulsive fixation on particular historical details which – considered in isolation – can never bear the burden of proof for the meaningfulness of divine providence. It is the whole of history (together with its faults and fractures) rather than particular details (for example the establishment of Constantine, the friend of Christianity, as sole ruler or the call of the Nicene Theodosius to be Augustus of the East), that is to be attributed to the one God – in truth an adventure of faith which cannot be based on certainty but only on hope. For from a Christian perspective, history is by no means a manifest victory parade by God through the world, but finds its image in the way of his incarnate Son to the cross – an image which discards the categories of victory and defeat, failure and success, because the surface reality alone cannot catch his true significance. Anyone who has the strength to see all history in this perspective will also not be too amazed or shaken by the questionable aspects of church politics. It is not the disputes, the interplay of power games and intrigues or the many indications of human narrowness that are astounding, but the fact that despite everything this chaos time and again opens up a glimpse of the depth dimensions of the (trinitarian) faith.

Here, too, it is the case that the decisive factor is not the terminological detail in itself – that the Neo-Nicene vocabulary is not immediately comprehensible today is no obstacle to its making important statements which can still be explained. Christian faith is about *one* and only *one* God, not about three Gods, however shaped or gradated, or about a Godhead 'divided into three'. Like all monothe-

istic religions, Christianity, too, derives reality from *a*
principle. It was the concern of the Monarchians, ⌐ᴵᴄ
Old Nicenes and especially also Marcellus of Ancyra, to
maintain this (albeit making it concrete in quite a different
way was also a concern of the Arians and after them the
Anhomoeans).

That this *one* God has revealed himself in salvation
history as Father, Son and Spirit is no ploy with mere names
(even if the biblical refractions in this revelation are intrinsically very diverse, as is evident for example in the divergent
christological perspectives of the New Testament), but shows
a true reality. The Eastern theology of the *three* hypostases
insists on this. The *one* God does not disguise himself in
salvation history but discloses how '*he himself*' is – namely
Father, Son and Holy Spirit. Salvation history is in truth the
self-revelation of God and not just a pedagogical measure to
teach human beings about something else.

To hold both the unity and trinity of God together was
the aim of the Neo-Nicene doctrine of the Trinity and will
remain the goal of any Christian theology if it wants to do
justice to the claim made by its own tradition and especially
by the early Christian councils. It can express that in other
words, but time and again it will have to keep the images
of the past before its eyes if it is not to end up in the same
'impasses'.

Those who see the saviour only as a creature (as did Arius
and his adherents, or earlier – in another manifestation
– the Adoptionist theologians) will have to face up to the
question of what notion of salvation they are representing.
The 'Nicene' horizon of salvation at any rate extends much
further than can be grasped with the categories of 'model'
(which would be given to us in any case in the life, teaching,
death and resurrection of Jesus) or even 'substitution' (in
the death of Jesus on the cross 'for our sins'). In Jesus
– according to the Nicene faith – we encounter the reality of
the true God, who unites his creation with himself, who not
only keeps it in being as creator (as Islam and Judaism also
confess) but enters into material reality and bears its burden
as his own – that is what the incarnation of the Logos means

– in order to change it from within through his Spirit and lead it to consummation. The saviour does not simply put the world 'in order' once again but draws it into God – from the 'Nicene' perspective that is the determination and goal of the universe from its first moment.

Those on the other side (such as the modalist Monarchians) who want to assume that in Jesus the Father himself has appeared as 'Son' will hardly be able to cope with the biblical witness or must regard salvation history (for example the depiction of the baptism of Jesus in the Jordan) as a kind of stage play in which the distinct 'roles' of the Father and the Son are 'acted out', because the Son is 'really' identical with the Father. The exegetes of the early church already saw that. Even today it is above all exegesis that makes a simplifying (Monarchian) view of the incarnation impossible. This throws us back on the question of authority and the truth-claim of the foundation documents of revelation. However much our insight into the time-conditioned nature of these documents and a sense of the plurality of the theological schemes offered in them and their possible interpretations may have developed, today we may not dispense with the task of establishing from the diversity of traditions the 'core content' of the biblical message (which also includes the Father really standing face to face with the Son) and preserving them from arbitrary transformations.

In that respect, in my view Neo-Nicene theology was successful, not because its exegesis was so convincing in every detail but because it found a viable way for its time of keeping the concerns of biblical monotheism in balance with the reality of Father, Son and Spirit which is also attested in the Bible, without locating the saviour and the consummator of the creation on the side of the creatures.

It says a lot for this theology that it is the result not of a *superficial* compromise (as the Homoean imperial dogma had been) but of *deepened* theological reflection in which an event such as the 'ecumenical consensus conversation' in Alexandria in 362 was of the utmost significance, because it documents the fundamental insight that terminology as such cannot be the touchstone of orthodoxy. Likewise, in

my view it is a strong point of the Neo-Nicene doct
the Trinity that it did not attempt to solve the prob
Christian 'extended' monotheism too rationalistically (as
Arius and even more the Anomoeans did), but set it within
the wider horizon of negative or apophatic theology. The
(Neo-)Arian statement that the only true God is without
origin or unbegotten is not of itself an expression of
authentic apophatic theology if this negative statement is
then immediately used affirmatively to 'define' the substance
of God. By contrast, the authentic apophatic theology of
the Cappadocians recalls that God is unfathomable in his
substance and cannot be reduced to a concept, cannot
be defined. That is not an evasion but shows the limits
of human 'images' of God. A finite spirit cannot grasp,
understand and think about the infinity of the living God,
far less express it. Therefore we remain dependent on
the testimony of the biblical revelation, which of course
expresses itself in human notions and words, and thus needs
interpretation – the Bible will not tolerate theological short
cuts. To this degree the Neo-Nicene view of the Trinity,
too, is not a 'logical' system that could be proved; rather, its
understanding of the biblical writings points to a mystery
which human beings can only approach time and again (in
different ways – not just through theological knowledge but
also through the liturgy or in personal spirituality) without
ever exhausting it.

God does not allow himself to be shut up in human
intellectual constructions. Those who want to encounter
him must be ready to maintain a search in which the early
church's dogma of the Trinity can point the direction. At
first glance that may seem meagre, but it is the only possibility of getting on the track of the truth – not of a myth, a
construct or an ideology.

Bibliography

This book is indebted to the specialist works listed below for many points of detail.

Brennecke, Hanns Christof, *Hilarius von Poitiers und die Bischofsopposition gegen Konstantius II. Untersuchungen zur dritten Phase des arianischen Streites (337-361)*, PTS 26, Berlin and New York 1984

id., *Studien zur Geschichte der Homöer. Der Osten bis zum Ende der homöischen Reichskirche*, BHTh 73, Tübingen 1988

Brox, Norbert, *Der Hirt des Hermas*, KAV 7, Göttingen 1991

Drecoll, Volker Henning, *Die Entwicklung der Trinitätslehre des Basilius von Cäsarea. Sein Weg vom Homöusianer zum Neonizäner*, FKDG 66, Göttingen 1996

Dünzl, Franz, *Pneuma. Funktionen des theologischen Begriffs in frühchristlicher Literatur*, JAC.E 30, Münster 2000

Field, Lester L., *On the Communion of Damasus and Meletius. Fourth-Century Synodal Formulae in the Codex Veronensis LX. With Critical Edition and Translation*, STPIMS 145, Toronto 2004

Hübner, Reinhard M., *Der paradox Eine. Antignostischer Monarchianismus im zweiten Jahrhundert. Mit einem Beitrag von Markus Vinzent*, SVigChr 50, Leiden, etc. 1999

Löhr, Winrich A., *Die Entstehung der homöischen und homöusianischen Kirchenparteien. Studien zur Synodalgeschichte des 4. Jahrhunderts*, BBKT 2, Witterschlick-Bonn 1986

Markschies, Christoph, *Ambrosius von Mailand und die Trinitätstheologie. Kirchen- und theologiegeschichtliche Studien zu Antiarianismus und Neunizänismus bei Ambrosius und im lateinischen Westen (364–381 n. Chr.)*, BHTh 90, Tübingen 1995

Opitz, Hans-Georg (ed.), *Athanasius Werke III/1. Urkunden zur Geschichte des Arianischen Streites*, Berlin 1935/1941

Ritter, Adolf-Martin, *Das Konzil von Konstantinopel und sein Symbol. Studien zur Geschichte und Theologie des II. Ökumenischen Konzils*, FKDG 15, Göttingen 1965

Seibt, Klaus, *Die Theologie des Markell von Ankyra*, AKG 59, Berlin and New York 1994

Ulrich, Jörg, *Die Anfänge der abendländischen Rezeption des Nizänums*, PTS 39, Berlin and New York 1994

Vinzent, Markus, 'Die Entstehung des "Römischen Glaubensbekenntnisses"', in Wolfram Kinzig, Christoph Markschies and Markus Vincent, *Tauffragen und Bekenntnis. Studien zur sogenannten 'Traditio Apostolica', zu den 'Interrogationes de fide' und zum 'Römischen Glaubensbekenntnis'*, AKG 74, Berlin and New York 1999, pp. 185–409

id. (ed. and trans.), *Markell von Ankyra – Die Fragmente. Der Brief an Julius von Rom*, SVigChr 39, Leiden, etc. 1997

Yeum, Changseon, *Die Synode von Alexandrien (362). Die dogmengeschichtliche und kirchenpolitische Bedeutung für die Kirche im 4. Jahrhundert*, Studien zur Orientalischen Kirchengeschichte 34, Münster 2005

Ziebritzki, Henning, *Heiliger Geist und Weltseele. Das Problem der dritten Hypostase bei Origenes, Plotin und ihren Vorläufern*, BHTh 84, Tübingen 1994

For Further Reading

Ayres, L., *Nicaea and its Legacy. An Approach to Fourth-Century Trinitarian Theology,* Oxford 2004

Barnard, L.W., *The Council of Serdica 343 AD,* Sofia 1983

Barnes, M.R. and Williams, D.H. (ed.), *Arianism after Arius, Essays on the Development of the Fourth Century Trinitarian Conflicts,* Edinburgh 1993

Ferguson, T.C., *The Past is Prologue. The Revolution of Nicene Historiography,* Leiden and Boston 2005

Gavrilyuk, P.L., *The Suffering of the Impassible God. The Dialectics of Patristic Thought,* Oxford 2004

Hanson, R.P.C., *The Search for the Christian Doctrine of God. The Arian Controversy 318-381,* Edinburgh 1988

Kelly, J.N.D., *Early Christian Creeds,* London and New York 1972

Kopecek, T.A., *A History of Neo-Arianism* (2 vols), Philadelphia 1979

Meredith, A., *The Cappadocians,* Crestwood, NJ 1995

Williams, D.H., *Ambrose of Milan and the End of the Nicene-Arian Conflict,* Oxford 1995

Williams, Rowan, *Arius. Heresy and Tradition,* reissued London and Grand Rapids 2001

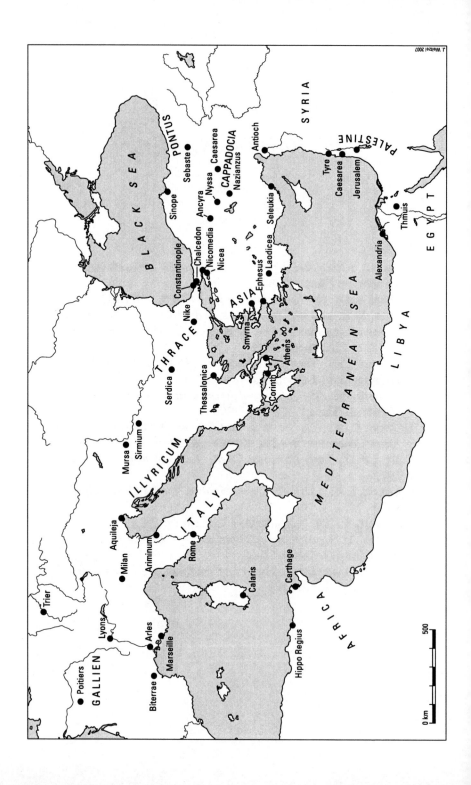

J. Weitzel 2007

Index

Lightning Source UK Ltd.
Milton Keynes UK
20 November 2010

163177UK00001B/113/P